LINGUISTICS

A Revolution in Teaching

Linguistics

A REVOLUTION IN TEACHING

Neil Postman
AND
Charles Weingartner

DELACORTE PRESS
NEW YORK

Library of Congress Catalog Card Number: 66-22201
Manufactured in the United States of America
First printing

ACKNOWLEDGMENT is made to the following authors, publishers and agents for permission to reprint excerpts from the following works:

William S. Beck, *Modern Science and the Nature of Life*. Reprinted by permission of Harcourt, Brace & World, Inc., and The Macmillan Co., Ltd.

G. Robert Carlsen, "*How* Do We Teach?" in *The English Journal*, 54, 5 (May 1965), pp. 364–369. Used by permission of the National Council of Teachers of English.

James B. Conant, *Modern Science and Modern Man*. Used by permission of Columbia University Press.

John B. Carroll, editor, *Language, Thought and Reality: Selected Writings of Benjamin Lee Whorf*. Used by permission of the M.I.T. Press, Cambridge, Massachusetts. Copyright 1956 by the Massachusetts Institute of Technology. All rights reserved.

Karl Dykema, "Historical Development of the Concept of Grammatical Properties" in *College Composition and Communication* (December 1954), pp. 135–140. Used by permission of the National Council of Teachers of English.

Eleanor Farjeon, "Jenny White and Johnny Black." From *Poems for Children* by Eleanor Farjeon. Copyright 1933, © 1961 by Eleanor Farjeon. Published by J. B. Lippincott Company. Reprinted by permission of J. B. Lippincott Company and Harold Ober Associates Incorporated.

Charles C. Fries, *American English Grammar*. Published by Appleton-Century. Used by permission of Charles C. Fries and the National Council of Teachers of English.

Erich Fromm, *May Man Prevail*. Copyright © 1961 by Erich Fromm. Reprinted by permission of the author.

John W. Gardner, *Self-Renewal*, pp. 21–23. Copyright © 1963, 1964 by John W. Gardner. Used by permission of Harper & Row, Publishers.

Marjorie Grene, "Portmann's Thought." Originally published in *Commentary*, November 1965. Used by permission of the author.

S. I. Hayakawa, "Linguistic Science and the Teaching of Composition." Reprinted from *ETC* by permission of the editors. Copyright 1950 by the International Society for General Semantics.

S. I. Hayakawa, "Semantics, Law, and Priestly-Minded Men." Reprinted from *ETC* by permission of the editors. Copyright © 1962 by the International Society for General Semantics.

Otto Jespersen, *Mankind, Nation, and Individual*. Used by permission of George Allen & Unwin, Ltd.

Wendell Johnson, *People in Quandries*, pp. 50–51. Copyright 1946 by Harper & Row, Publishers, Incorporated. Used by permission of the publishers.

Franz Kafka, *The Great Wall of China*. Reprinted by permission of Schocken Books, Inc., from *The Great Wall of China* by Franz Kafka. Copyright © 1946, 1948 by Schocken Books, Inc. Reprinted by permission of Martin Secker & Warburg Ltd.

Jean Malmstrom and Annabel Ashley, *Dialects U.S.A.* (Champaign, Ill.: National Council of Teachers of English, 1963), pp. 11–13. Used by permission of the National Council of Teachers of English.

W. Somerset Maugham, *The Summing Up*. Copyright 1938 by W. Somerset Maugham. Reprinted by permission of Doubleday & Company, Inc., the Literary Executor of the Estate of the Late Mr. W. Somerset Maugham, and William Heinemann, Ltd.

Karl Menninger, M.D., *The Vital Balance*. Copyright © 1963 by Karl Menninger, M.D. Reprinted by permission of The Viking Press.

The New York Times, three articles appearing September 27, 1962, and November 18, 1961. Copyright © 1961 and 1962 by The New York Times Company. Reprinted by permission.

Neil Postman and Howard C. Damon, *The Languages of Discovery*. Reprinted by special permission of the publisher, Holt, Rinehart and Winston, Inc., from *The Languages of Discovery* by Neil Postman and Howard C. Damon. Copyright © 1965.

Neil Postman, *Exploring Your Language*. Reprinted by special permission of the publisher, Holt, Rinehart and Winston, Inc., from *Exploring Your Language* by Neil Postman. Copyright © 1966.

I. A. Richards, *Interpretation and Teaching*. Used by permission of Harcourt, Brace & World, Inc., and Routledge & Kegan Paul Ltd.

I. A. Richards, *Practical Criticism*. Used by permission of Harcourt, Brace & World, Inc., and Routledge & Kegan Paul Ltd.

I. A. Richards and C. K. Ogden, *The Meaning of Meaning*. Used by permission of Harcourt, Brace & World, Inc., and Routledge & Kegan Paul Ltd.

Bertrand Russell, *The Impact of Science on Society*. Used by permission of Simon and Schuster, Inc., and George Allen & Unwin Ltd.

James W. Sabol, "An Experiment with Inductive Language Study," from *Patterns and Models for Teaching English*, 1964. Reprinted with the permission of the National Council of Teachers of English and James W. Sabol.

Carl Sandburg, "Languages," from *Chicago Poems* by Carl Sandburg. Copyright 1916 by Holt, Rinehart and Winston, Inc. Copyright 1944 by Carl Sandburg. Reprinted by permission of Holt, Rinehart and Winston, Inc., Jonathan Cape Limited, and Laurence Pollinger Limited.

Mikhail Sholokov, *And Quiet Flows the Don*. Copyright 1934 by Alfred A. Knopf, Inc. Translated by Stephen Garry. Used by permission of Alfred A. Knopf, Inc., and Putnam & Company Ltd.

Gore Vidal, "Passage to Egypt." Reprinted by permission of *Esquire* Magazine. Copyright © 1962 by Esquire, Inc.

Alan Watts, *The Way of Zen*. Copyright © 1957 by Pantheon Books. Reprinted by permission of Random House, Inc.

Encyclopedia of Educational Research. Used by permission of The Macmillan Company.

Acknowledgment is also made to LaRuth Gray, Alan Criswell, Alan Shapiro, Jane Morrisey and Ray Arlo for permission to use their material.

CONTENTS

PREFATORY REMARKS

THERE IS A STORY told in the *Shabbat* about the famous Jewish scholar Rabbi Hillel which has some pertinence to the text before you. Hillel was asked by a colleague if he could teach the Torah in the time he could stand on one leg. He replied: "What is hateful to thee, do not do unto thy fellow man. That is the whole doctrine. The rest is mere commentary."

We are aware of the risks in using this story here. Allow us, therefore, to disclaim at once any implication that our book is a sacred text, or that the authors rival Hillel in wisdom and economy of expression. We cite the story because it illuminates two aspects of our book. The first concerns the need for the book; the second, the way in which the book is organized.

First, to the need: Linguistics is here to stay. Along with the "new math," the "new science," and the "new social studies," linguistics is increasingly affecting what is done to children in school. As professors of English Education and as executive officers of The Linguistics Demonstration Center at New York University, we have had occasion to talk with hundreds of teachers and scores of parents concerned about new developments in the teaching of English. Although what they have had to say has varied in tone and depth, almost all of them shared some sense of confusion about linguistics. Once, when we asked a young English teacher how she would define linguistics, she said, "Linguistics is English sentences with numbers above each word." A member of the PTA told us on another occasion that so far as he was concerned, linguistics is "the same old stuff with new terminology." (Considering what was going on in his daughter's school, he was probably right!) In most cases, however, teachers and parents have been more interrogative than declarative (or accusative). What is linguistics? they want to know. Who are linguists? What is linguistics good for in the schools? Can it help children to write better? To read with greater comprehension? To speak or listen more effectively? When these questions have been put to us, we have most often referred the questioners to available books and articles, sometimes even our own. But the procedure was not wholly adequate, it turned out, because after reading the books and articles, the questioners frequently returned, still wanting to know what linguistics is and what in the world it is good for, if anything. It sometimes seemed to us that the only answers they would accept are those that can be given in the time it takes to stand on one leg. Brevity, they wanted. Economy. Words of one syllable. If the teachings of the Torah can be stated in a sentence, surely someone can do the same for linguistics. We decided to accept the challenge. But lacking Rabbi Hillel's simplicity and economy, we did the next best thing: We wrote a book. But not a long book. And a book written as simply and clearly as we could, intended for teachers and laymen who are asking questions about linguistics similar to the ones we have mentioned.

Now, to the organization of the book: If we may paraphrase Rabbi Hillel, the first three chapters present the basic message; the rest is mere commentary. In Chapters 1, 2, and 3 we try to answer the questions, What is linguistics? What do linguists do? and What is linguistics good for? If you do not get beyond these chapters, you will at least know what our answers are and why we give them.

If you should go beyond these chapters, here is what you will find: six chapters, each dealing with a particular field of linguistic inquiry. Each attempts to describe briefly the kinds of inquiries linguists have made in that field and some of the results they have produced. In addition, each chapter includes detailed accounts of some of the important educational (i.e., mostly classroom) applications of linguistics. In this way, we hope to contribute toward changing the title of our book from a prediction to a description.

NEIL POSTMAN
CHARLES WEINGARTNER

New York City, 1966

PART ONE

CHAPTER 1

What Is Linguistics?

> I have said something at several places . . . about the peculiar paralysis which the mention of definitions and, still more, the discussion of them induces. It can be prevented, I believe, by stressing the purposive aspect of definitions. We want to do something and a definition is a means of doing it. If we want certain results, then we must use certain meanings (or definitions). But no definition has any authority apart from a purpose, or to bar us from other purposes. And yet they endlessly do so. Who can doubt that we are often deprived of very useful thoughts merely because the words which might express them are being temporarily preempted by other meanings? Or that a development is often frustrated merely because we are sticking to a former definition of no service to the new purpose?
>
> —I. A. RICHARDS, *Interpretation in Teaching*

We need hardly say that any definition of linguistics (or of anything else, for that matter) depends on who is doing the defining. But a point worth considering is why this should be so. Definitions vary largely because definers have different purposes. As I. A. Richards suggests in the quotation above, it is both sensible and liberating to define a definition as a verbal strategy designed to help achieve an objective. A definition seen in this way is something to build with—a blueprint that gives direction to our activities. This is another way of saying that there is no "real" or "true" definition of linguistics, just as there is no "real" or "true" definition of psychology, or philosophy, or history. The questions to ask of a definition are not Is it true? or Is it real? but, What does this definition allow me to see? What does it prevent me from seeing? What lines of inquiry does it allow me to follow? In short, we must always bear in mind that a definition is an instrument which helps us do our thinking and accomplish our purposes.

Although we shall have occasion to allude to several different and highly useful definitions of linguistics later, it is important that you understand from the beginning that the purpose of the definition we shall stress is to help improve the teaching of English in our schools. Our definition is a strategy for translating linguistics into programs and attitudes that can make the study of English a more relevant and useful activity than it has been. The problem of instruction, as John Dewey insisted, is to provide students with *something to do* that will engage their imaginations and heighten their capacity to conduct inquiries. The definition we offer is intended to contribute toward this goal. At the same time, it has wide acceptance among professional linguists, who, guided by it, have produced an impressive variety of questions, answers, and theories.

What, then, is linguistics?

Linguistics is a way of behaving. It is an activity, a process of doing something. More specifically, it is a way of behaving while one attempts to discover information and to acquire knowledge about language. The information and knowledge that result from such inquiry-behavior become part of what is meant by linguistics. But it would be a mistake to define linguistics as a body of specific assertions about language. Facts, or even theories, by themselves are not linguistics, just as facts or theories alone are not science. "Science is a pursuit," Dewey once wrote, "not a coming into possession of the immutable." To which Ernest Nagel adds: "The history of science makes amply clear that the method of science is a more permanent part of the scientific enterprise than are most of the substantive conclusions asserted at any given time." In other words, the facts of genetics in 1935 may be different from the facts of genetics in 1960, but what remains essentially unchanged and continually productive is the behavior, the activity, the pursuit that we call the *scientific method.*

This view of general science is precisely our view of linguistic science. The facts of linguistic science in 1935 may be different from the facts of linguistic science in 1960, which in turn may be different from the facts of linguistic science in 1980. But what remain essentially unchanged and continually productive are the processes of inquiry that we define as *linguistics* or, if you will, the *linguistic enterprise.*

What are the characteristics of the linguistic enterprise? First, and most important, linguistics requires that the student of language adopt certain attitudes. Unless one agrees to these, one cannot participate in the linguistic enterprise. They include (1) a hostility toward dogmatism and authoritarianism, (2) an understanding that all answers are tentative, (3) a willingness to accept the possibility that there may exist different and even conflicting answers to the same question, and (4) a preference for objectivity and detachment. Although this list can be extended, the statements above constitute the basic imperatives of the scientific frame of mind. For this reason, a few general observations about these attitudes need to be made.

First, it is much easier to describe the scientific frame of mind than to use it. Even professional scientists do not always have an easy time predicating their behavior on such attitudes, particularly if they are not accustomed to using them in their nonprofessional life. Discipline is required and probably at some time, in some situation, confronted by some particular problem, every scientist has failed to provide himself with the needed discipline.

Second, the attitudes that characterize the scientific enterprise are identical with those that are normally a precondition of intellectual and emotional growth. In other words, although these attitudes are adopted consciously for specialized purposes by scientists, they may serve as the basis of a general point of view that will help anyone to continue learning. This point is one we will come back to again and again, since one of education's basic challenges is to help students learn how to learn, not simply in specific disciplines but also in unsystematized areas of life.

For example, the scientific attitude stresses adaptability. Adaptability is a recognition of, and a way of responding to, the fact that the world and all that's in it, including knowledge, are not static but are undergoing continual processes of change. How many of our own personal problems, not to mention the world's problems, could be alleviated if each of us were more adaptable? How many of us are blocked from learning because of beliefs that have become fixed? To what extent do we make ourselves obsolete by failing to adapt to new conditions? It is surely not too much to suggest that one's education should increase rather than reduce one's "adaptability quotient."

Third, scientific attitudes are held to be entirely agreeable when they are used in such pursuits as biology, physics, and astronomy, but they are apt to be considered offensive when stringently adopted in the social sciences, particularly in the study of language. Most of us have an emotional commitment to the ways in which we use language that often prevents us from exhibiting, say, an appropriate objectivity and detachment. We sometimes insist, for example, on maintaining definitions (say, of "good English" or "correct grammar") that the language scientist may find useless. Or we may object to a certain *descriptive* statement because it reveals language changes of which we do not approve. As Leonard Bloomfield wrote in *Language:*

> Many people have difficulty at the beginning of language study, not in grasping the methods or results (which are simple enough), but in stripping off the preconceptions which are forced on us by our popular-scholastic doctrine.

Whatever the source of the preconceptions, there is no denying that some of the hostility that linguistics has aroused is attributable to the discomfort that accompanies the application of the scientific attitude to intimate aspects of behavior.

Of course, the way of behaving we call linguistics involves

more than the adoption of certain attitudes. There are specific procedures that need to be followed. These procedures—they are perhaps better thought of as guidelines—are not as well known by the general public as are the attitudes of science, although one might argue that such guidelines are used quite commonly by most people in everyday practical affairs. Thomas Henry Huxley wrote, "The method of scientific investigation is nothing but the expression of the necessary mode of working of the human mind." Huxley may be right insofar as he is talking about a mind that is *working,* but it is a melancholy fact that too frequently most of us do not engage our minds in inquiry processes. Those who do, recognize at least six steps:

1. *The defining process.* This process refers to the scientist's attempt to insure that he will talk sense. We do not imply that semantic rigor, or clarity of definition, is always the first step in the inquiry process. Sometimes the nature of the problem causes it to occur later. But in most cases, inquiry into a particular problem cannot proceed very far until the inquirer has made clear to himself (and preferably others) the meanings of the key terms and concepts involved in his work. For example, linguists have provided quite specific meanings for such terms as *language, grammar, dialect,* and *usage,* meanings that are at variance with the conventional understanding of these terms, but that are far more precise. These meanings are designed by linguists to serve specific purposes, and their value can only be judged by determining how well the definitions help the linguist to accomplish his work. The term *linguistics* itself, as we have already suggested, has been differently (and resourcefully) defined by linguists because, as usual, each definer has wanted to accomplish different things.

We must leave it to the reader to decide how much of a nuisance is the inevitable proliferation of technical terms in linguistics or any other science. Suffice it to say that the development of a precise vocabulary is more than an adjunct to science; it is a necessary condition for the conduct of scientific inquiry. As Wendell Johnson observes in *People in Quandaries,* "The language of science is the better part of the method of science."

Scientific method requires, above all, that language be used in a responsible way. To define "responsible" for you, we quote Johnson again:

> There is a cardinal principle in terms of which language is used scientifically: It must be used meaningfully. The statements made must refer directly or indirectly (by means of interrelated definitions) to something in the realm of experience. It is not enough that they refer to something for the speaker and that they also refer to something for the listener. What is required is that they refer to approximately the same thing for both the speaker and the listener. In speaking meaningfully one does not just communicate; one communicates something to someone. And the something communicated is not the words that are used, but whatever those words represent. The degree to which communication occurs depends precisely upon the degree to which the words represent the same thing for the listener that they do for the speaker. And the degree to which they do is an index of the clarity that is such a basic feature of scientific language. . . .
>
> Clarity is so important in the language of science . . . because clarity is a prerequisite to validity. It is to be considered that statements that "flow beautifully" and are grammatically superb may be also devoid of factual meaning, or meaningful but vague, or precise but invalid. Now, scientific statements . . . must be both clear and valid. They can be clear without having validity, but if they are unclear their validity cannot well be determined. They must then, first of all, be clear or factually meaningful; they must be that before the question of their validity can even be raised. We ask, "What do you mean?" before we ask, "How do you know?" Until we reach agreement as to precisely what a person is talking about, we cannot possibly reach agreement as to whether or in what degree his statements are true.

The particular importance of the language of linguistics can be seen even when such naive questions as the following are posed, all of which have been addressed to the authors by students: What people speak the best English? Is *irregardless* a word? Isn't English a better language than Russian? What does *disinterested* really mean? Whose grammar is better—mine or his?

Before one can begin to provide "answers" to such questions, one must know what the questioner means. What, for example, is meant by "good English" or "grammar" or "a word" or "really"? For some people (perhaps most) "good English" may mean language that is approved by English teachers or dictionaries. For others, it may mean language that is characterized by polysyllabic words and intricate syntax. During a recent mayoralty campaign in New York City, the authors heard a citizen praise one of the candidates, William Buckley, Jr., by saying, "I didn't understand what he said, but he certainly uses good English." The point is: A scientist cannot afford to assume that the same meanings are given by everyone to even the most common words—indeed, *especially* to the most common words.

Thus, among the earliest steps in the method of scientific inquiry is the development of a way of talking that will insure a high degree of communicability, a way that will permit others to determine the validity of one's statements. Naturally, a basic element in this "way of talking" is the maintenance of a more or less rigid distinction among different kinds of statements. Linguists largely confine themselves to making *factual* statements (i.e., statements capable of objective verification), or *inferential* statements (i.e., statements about the unknown based on the known, and therefore susceptible to indirect methods of validation). They try to avoid making what are called *value judgments* (i.e., expressions of what is good and beautiful or bad and ugly), and equally to avoid *exhortations* or *prescriptive statements* (i.e., advice on what people ought to do). All of which leads to the second step in the linguistic enterprise.

2. *The questioning process.* For a great many years now, most linguists have refused to consider the question, How and where did language originate? Their reason is that the data

needed to answer are not accessible (are, in fact, hardly imaginable). Thus, they tend to view this kind of question as not meaningful. This does not imply that such questions are not worth asking for nonscientific purposes. They may, for example, inspire the writing of an epic novel on Neanderthal man. But within the framework of the scientific enterprise, such questions are rejected because they suggest no procedures, inquiries, or observations that a scientist can conduct. When relevant operations *can* be imagined, such questions will be assigned an entirely different status from that which they now have. Quite apart from the issues involved in origin-of-language questions, it must be understood that any scientist works hard at posing clear questions to which answers can be found. In brief, he accepts several assumptions about the question-asking process:

a. He assumes that the terminology of the question determines the terminology of the answer. (For example, if he allows the vague term "better" to go undefined in the question "Is English a better language than Russian?" he can expect only an equally vague and perhaps meaningless answer.)

b. He assumes that a question cannot be answered unless there are procedures by which reliable answers can be obtained. (For example, what procedures would one employ to answer these questions: How many angels can dance on the head of a pin? Is language a divine inspiration? Or, to take a question that *seems* more sensible, Which is better, an inflected language or an analytic language?)

c. He assumes that the value of a question is to be determined not only by the specificity and richness of the answers it produces, but also by the quantity and quality of the new questions it suggests. (In other words, he asks, "What can I *do* with the answers? What lines of inquiry do they suggest I follow?")

3. *The observing process*. In "Linguists and the Sense of Mission," Allen Walker Read states: "The collection of impartial, unbiased observations is the first step in linguistics." (Of course, Professor Read is taking for granted the first two

stages described above. For our purposes, we could not afford a similar economy.) In any case, it is certainly true that *observation* is an early and basic phase of the linguistic "way of behaving." Observation is, in fact, an early and basic phase of all scientific investigations, and is at the center of what is called the *inductive method of inquiry*.

There are many ways to describe the inductive method, and not all of the differences among the descriptions are trivial. Nonetheless, the cardinal rule of all inductive procedures is that statements of fact must be based on observation, not on unsupported authority, "logical" conclusions, or personal or collective preferences. "To modern educated people," Bertrand Russell writes, "it seems obvious that matters of fact are to be ascertained by observation, not by consulting ancient authorities. But this is an entirely modern conception, which hardly existed before the seventeenth century. Aristotle maintained that women have fewer teeth than men; although he was twice married, it never occurred to him to verify his statement by examining his wives' mouths. He said also that children will be healthier if conceived when the wind is in the north. One gathers that the two Mrs. Aristotles both had to run and look at the weathercock every evening before going to bed. He states that a man bitten by a mad dog will not go mad, but any other animal will (*Hist. An.* 704*a*); that the bite of the shrewmouse is dangerous to horses, especially if the mouse is pregnant (604*b*); that elephants suffering from insomnia can be cured by rubbing their shoulders with salt, olive oil, and warm water (605*a*); and so on and so on."

This quotation interests us for several reasons, least of which is that it calls into question Aristotle's reputation as an astute observer. What is of greatest interest is that in the area of language most "modern educated people" may still rely more on "ancient authorities" than they do on observations—their own or those of someone else. Why this should be so has much to do with the fact that some things are believed because people feel that they *should* be true or that they *need* to be true. An excellent description of this way of thinking is provided by Mikhail Sholokov in *And Quiet Flows the Don*. In this passage, Chikamasov discusses with his friend Bunchuk the question of Lenin's origins:

> "Bunchuk, what race is Lenin from? I mean where was he born and grew up?"
>
> "Lenin? He's a Russian."
>
> "Ho?"
>
> "It's true; he's a Russian."
>
> "No, brother, you're wrong there. It's clear you don't know much about him," Chikamasov said with a touch of superiority in his voice. "Do you know where he's from? He's of our blood. He's come from the Don Cossacks, and was born in Salskov province. . . . understand? They say he was in the army as an artillery-man. And his face fits: he's like the lower Cossacks—strong cheekbones and the same eyes."
>
> "How do you know?"
>
> "The Cossacks have talked it over among themselves, and I've heard so."
>
> "No, Chikamasov, he's a Russian, and was born in Simbirak province."
>
> "I don't believe you. And it's very simple why. There's Pugachov; was he a Cossack? And Stenka Razin? And Timofievich Yermak? That's it! There's not a man who has ever raised the poor people against the Tsar who wasn't a Cossack. And you say he was from a Siberian province! I'm ashamed to hear such words, Ilia."

Chikamasov's reasoning is easy to follow. Lenin is a Cossack because (1) the Cossacks in Chikamasov's regiment have talked it over and decided that he is; (2) Pugachov, Razin, and Yermak—all revolutionaries—were Cossacks, and since Lenin is a revolutionary, he too must be a Cossack; and, finally, (3) because Chikamasov wishes Lenin to be a Cossack.

It would be relatively easy to imagine a conversation involving similar reasoning about a fact of language. Such "conversations" probably occur hundreds of times a day in English classrooms throughout the country. The difference is that if there are any Bunchuks in the room—that is, people who have the facts—they are most likely too intimidated or uninterested to oppose the Chikamasovs.

Linguistics, then, requires observations. What kinds of observations? The answer to this question depends on what the linguist is trying to do, and these matters will be dealt with in a general way in the next chapter and specifically in Part Two, where various branches of linguistics are discussed. However, it is necessary here to point out that there are largely two kinds of data that linguists seek. One concerns language itself—its forms, its sounds, its shapes, its changes, its varieties, its rules. The second concerns the effects of language on people; for example, How does language affect or reflect our assumptions, our attitudes, our perceptions, our prejudices, our evaluations, our behavior? Whatever kinds of inquiries they are conducting—and the variety is much greater than is generally supposed—linguists accept the assumption that (to quote Leonard Bloomfield) "the only useful generalizations about language are inductive generalizations."

4. *The classifying process.* Insofar as possible, the linguist tries to invent classification systems that are reasonably objective and consistent. The problems this process poses for linguists vary in difficulty according to the nature of the data they must deal with. "We could not use a telephone directory," Bloomfield wrote, "which arranged the names of the subscribers not in their alphabetical order, but according to some nonverbal characteristic, such as weight, height, or generosity." Thus, Bloomfield developed a useful taxonomy, for grammarians, based on the forms of language. Some have maintained that the major contribution of the grammar known as structural linguistics is that it provides a distinctive, consistent, and objective system of classification of "parts of speech." They maintain, further, that this being its main contribution, structural linguistics produces trivial insights into language. Without our arguing this matter here, it is important to observe that *every* language inquirer needs either to use some established system or invent his own in order to arrange his data in a useful and objective way.

For example, English usage is traditionally placed in one of two categories, "good English" and "bad English." But some linguists have found that their data do not lend themselves to division into two categories, especially ones with such moralistic connotations. They have accordingly used "Acceptable," "Disputable," "Vulgate"; or "Formal," "Colloquial," "Slang"; or five categories, or six. All of this may be awkward for those who want quick answers to practical questions, but the linguist must be governed by the integrity of his data. What he aims at is categorizing in a manner that will produce agreement on the placement of data once the criteria for placement are known. If the grammarian comes closer to achieving this than other linguists, it is because his data lend themselves to more objective classification. In fact, grammar has been called a "taxonomic science," that is, largely concerned with the classification of language data. Nonetheless, all linguists struggle with the problem of classification, and sometimes are prevented from coming to useful conclusions until they have found an adequate organizational principle.

5. *The generalizing process.* The collection of data and their orderly arrangement must eventually lead to the formulation of a generalization, or hypothesis, "rule," or "law." As Albert Einstein wrote, "It is the aim of science to establish general rules which determine the reciprocal connections between objects and events in time and space." In other words, one must first carefully observe objects and events; after having done so, one must state certain rules or laws that will explain their connections. This is what is meant here by the generalizing process. Are there "laws" that explain the sound changes that take place in language over periods of time? Are there general "rules" that explain how we formulate English sentences? Are there "principles" that determine whether language will produce cooperation or hostility? Can a hypothesis be stated about the connection between perception and the structure of language? Is it possible to state the general conditions that result in "misreading"? Or the general conditions that produce "effective" writing?

Obviously, these questions are not only at different levels of abstraction but are also at different points on the road to resolution. Moreover, we have not drawn adequate distinctions among such terms as "law," "rule," "principle," "hypothesis," and "generalization," some of which distinctions are esoteric, or at least extremely technical. Our purpose is only to stress that an important goal of all inductive inquiry is to use observed facts as the basis for moving to some higher-order abstraction about the facts. In turn, the purpose of formulating such generalizations is to make reliable predictions about the objects and events one has observed. Certainly one of the fundamental tests of the validity of a generalization is whether or not the generalization is useful in making reliable predictions.

It must be pointed out, however, that not all "sciences" put equal stress on prediction as a basis for validating generalizations. Geology and archaeology, for example, seek largely to reconstruct past events, and are not usually thought of as predictive sciences. Some of the theories, laws, and rules of linguistic science can be used as a basis for predicting future events, but many are useful only as hypotheses about what probably happened in the past, or is happening now.

6. *The verifying and revising process.* Ideally, the scientist does not defend his theories, laws, and generalizations. He tests them. And, if necessary, revises them. As Wendell Johnson reminds us, the scientist would rather be right than steadfast. (He'd rather switch than fight.) Stated simply, the linguist is required, as are other scientists, to seek verification of the generalizations that are the result of his inquiries. He must guard against developing a proprietary interest in any particular point of view, for he may have to abandon a hypothesis when new data fail to support it. Included in our conception of the verifying and revising process is the possibility that the linguist may have to abandon a particular point of view not only because the available data do not warrant it, but because the point of view does not reveal "significant" information or suggest "significant" ideas. For example, one of the persistent charges of the "*very* new" grammarians (i.e., transformational) against the "new" grammarians (i.e., structural linguists) is that the generalizations of the latter, while largely true, are

so obvious that they are scarcely worth serious thought. Without our discussing this argument here (we shall in Chap. 4), it should be noted that the major difference between the "new" grammarians and the "*very* new" grammarians is in the kinds of questions they ask, and when grammarians do change from one point of view to another they are usually motivated by their conviction that one set of problems is more significant than another.

The six processes described above are the basic guidelines for the conduct of scientific inquiry, and when they are applied to the study of language they define the linguistic enterprise. Each of the processes is capable of almost infinite refinement; in fact, the task of refining just one of them can occupy a linguist's entire career. In other words, not *all* linguists use *all* of these procedures during the course of a particular investigation, or even during the course of their professional lives. A linguist may devote himself for many years solely to the task of formulating useful questions, or to making a certain lexicon more precise, or to devising more sensitive techniques for collecting data, or to collecting data. What is important is that his behavior reflect, in a general way, his understanding and acceptance of the attitudes and procedures we have indicated.

What is Linguistics? It is conducting oneself in a particular manner—a scientific manner—when studying language.

CHAPTER 2

What Do Linguists Do?

LINGUISTICS, we have said, is conducting yourself in a particular manner—a scientific manner—when you study language. But what exactly are linguists interested in studying? What are the aspects of language and language behavior which have come under investigation by men who are called linguists? After all, most disciplines are concerned in some way with language problems. Are anthropologists linguists? Are psychologists linguists? Are philosophers? Literary critics? Engineers? Physicists? Our answer is, They are *when they are using scientific procedures to inquire into the role of language in human affairs.* In fact, some of the great contributors to the linguistic enterprise have conducted their inquiries from a background of other disciplines. For example: Sapir and Whorf from anthropology, I. A. Richards from literary criticism, Korzybski from engineering, Bridgman from physics, Piaget from psychology, Russell and Wittgenstein from philosophy. This roster of important linguists may come as a surprise to those who tend to view linguistics as (almost solely) an activity of grammarians. But linguistics is far too important a process to be left entirely or even principally in the hands of grammarians, as we shall have occasion to discuss in a moment.

By considering some of the definitions of linguistics offered by important language-inquirers, we can achieve some understanding of the variety of studies made by men who form part of the community of linguistic scholars.

One ought to begin with Leonard Bloomfield, generally regarded as the most important figure in linguistics in this century. In his book *Language* (first published in 1914), Bloomfield defines linguistics as the study of language in a scientific way. By defining linguistics as a process of inquiry (as we have), Bloomfield meant to allow (as we would) a broad scope to investigators, and his book reveals the wide range of subjects he felt to be legitimate areas of investigation. He includes discussions of phonology (sound systems), grammatical forms, syntax, dialect geography, language history, and language change.

One of Bloomfield's great colleagues in the development of linguistics was Edward Sapir, whose background was largely in anthropology. In a speech delivered in 1928 at a joint meeting of the Linguistic Society of America, the American Anthropological Association, and the American Association for the Advancement of Science, Sapir urged linguists to become aware of what their science may mean for the interpretation of human conduct in general. "It is difficult for a modern linguist to confine himself to his traditional subject matter," Sapir said, meaning by traditional subject matter comparative and historical studies. "Unless he is somewhat unimaginative," Sapir continued, "he cannot but share in some or all of the mutual interests which tie up linguistics with anthropology and culture history, with sociology, with psychology, with philosophy, and, more remotely, with physics and physiology." Sapir thus staked out an even wider field for linguists than perhaps Bloomfield was willing to do. (Bloomfield, for example, strongly cautioned against linguists associating themselves with certain "schools of psychology.")

Sapir's most distinguished student, Benjamin Lee Whorf, took his teacher's remarks to heart, and redefined linguistics in a way that would permit the exploration of untouched areas of language. In an article written in 1936, titled "A Linguistic Consideration of Thinking in Primitive Communities," Whorf wrote:

> The ethnologist engaged in studying a living primitive culture must often have wondered: What do these people think? How do they think? Are their intellectual and rational processes akin to ours or radically different? But thereupon he has probably dismissed the idea as a psy-

> chological enigma and has sharply turned his attention back to more readily observable matters. And yet the problem of thought and thinking in the native community is not purely and simply a psychological problem. It is quite largely cultural. It is moreover largely a matter of . . . language. It is approachable through linguistics, and, as I hope to show, the approach requires a rather new type of emphasis in linguistics, now beginning to emerge through the work of Sapir, Leonard Bloomfield, and others. . . . What needs to be clearly seen by anthropologists, who to a large extent may have gotten the idea that linguistics is merely a highly specialized and tediously technical pigeonhole in a far corner of the anthropological workshop, is that linguistics is essentially the quest of meaning. It may seem to the outsider to be inordinately absorbed in recording hair-splitting distinctions of sound, performing phonetic gymnastics, and writing complex grammars which only grammarians read. But the simple fact is that its real concern is to light up the thick darkness of the language, and thereby of much of the thought, the culture, and the outlook upon life of a given community.

Whorf's studies of exotic languages, notably the language of the Hopi Indians of Arizona, eventually led to the formulation of what is still the most provocative hypothesis in the linguistic enterprise: the idea that the structure of the language one habitually uses influences the manner in which one perceives and understands his environment.

To Whorf, linguistics is essentially "the quest of meaning." To I. A. Richards, "General Linguistic," as he calls it, is a similar quest, although his particular search took him to different materials and challenged him to look for different things. In *Practical Criticism,* published in 1929, Richards wrote:

> It is the oddest thing about language, whose history is full of odd things (and one of the oddest facts about human development) that so few people ever sat down to reflect systematically about meaning. For no daring or original steps are needed to carry our acquaintance with these

> matters at least one step further than the stage at which it usually remains. A little pertinacity and a certain habit of examining our intellectual and emotional instruments as we use them, is all that is required. From the point of view thus attained one would expect that our libraries would be full of works on the theory of interpretation, the diagnosis of linguistic situations, systematic ambiguity and the function of complex symbols; and that there would be Chairs of Significs or of General Linguistic at all our Universities. Yet, in point of fact, there is no respectable treatise on the theory of linguistic interpretation in existence, and no person whose professional occupation it is to inquire into these questions and direct study in the matter. For grammatical studies do not trespass upon this topic. Surely systematic investigation of the uses of language may be expected to improve our actual daily use of it, at least in the same measure that the study of plant-physiology may improve agriculture or human physiology assist medicine or hygiene.

By quoting Sapir, Whorf, and Richards at some length, we have run the risk of losing your interest. But not without good reason. It is extremely important that the concerns of linguists be seen as covering a very wide field. Whorf's and Richard's remarks about the limitations of grammar are germane. In our view, it would be a disaster if linguistics became identified solely with inquiries into grammatical problems, a disaster not only for the vitality of the discipline, but particularly for the teaching of English. And yet, if our communications with teachers of English are an indication, linguistics has already become for many simply a synonym for "new grammars" or "new theories of grammar." Such a state of affairs parallels the belief held by some that psychiatry is synonymous with psychoanalysis. The identification of linguistics with grammar has probably occurred because so many linguists of more recent vintage than Bloomfield, Sapir, Whorf, and Richards have confined their inquiries to grammar. Their definitions of linguistics therefore reflect their limited perspective. "Linguistics is the study of the internal structure of language," goes one. "Linguistics is the scientific study of the structure of sentences," goes another. "The task of linguistics is to produce adequate grammatical theories" is still another.

We must emphasize that insofar as such definitions help linguists to focus their attention on special aspects of language, there can be no objection to them. Definitions such as these have produced a wealth of reliable data, provocative questions, and imaginative theories about grammar. In some ways, grammar is the most active (even if not the most interesting) field in the linguist's terrain. But the equation of linguistics and grammar not only excludes the work of major language scholars; it also sharply diminishes the relevance of linguistics to the study and teaching of English. As we remarked in the first chapter, we wish to stress a conception of linguistics that (1) has a high status among linguists themselves, and (2) provides the greatest possible utility for the work of the schools.

What, then, are the subject matters of linguistics? How, in fact, have linguists of varying interests and backgrounds collectively defined the "role of language in human affairs"?

Without claiming to be exhaustive, we list below, along with brief explanations, aspects of language and language behavior that have attracted the attention of linguists. (At the back of this book is a chart that tries to provide for your convenience a picture of the total field of linguistics. In Part Two, there are detailed descriptions of the work of linguists in several fields.)

As Bloomfield indicated, the *phonology* (sounds), *morphology* (word forms), and *syntax* (phrases and sentences) of languages are legitimate areas of investigation for linguists. The inquiries made are of two kinds, descriptive and historical. For example, there is the question, "What were (or are) the significant sounds of a language at a specific time (including now)? There is also the question, "What are the patterns or dynamics of change in the sound system of a language over a period of time?" The second type of question—the historical—was asked frequently by linguists in the nineteenth century, when they called themselves comparative philologists. The first type of question has been more frequently asked in this century by men calling themselves descriptive linguists. Inquiries by both kinds of linguists have produced studies in *language history,* in which questions about the origins of words and the relationships among languages have been studied.

As Bloomfield also indicated, *dialect geography* is another area of investigation. The data sought here concern the variations of pronunciation, syntax, and vocabulary among the regional dialects of a language. Such inquiries may also focus on the language variations among different economic and social classes and vocational groups, although the term *linguistic sociology* would perhaps be more appropriate for these studies.

Usage denotes inquiries into the attitudes of speakers of a language toward certain words and structures. In other words, the linguist tries to find out what kind of social status certain pronunciations, grammatical forms, and expressions have among different groups.

Lexicography refers generally to the process of compiling dictionaries. Lexicographers are mainly concerned with inquiring into the meanings as well as the pronunciations, grammatical functions, history, and spellings of words. Of course they rely heavily on studies in *usage, dialect geography,* and *language history* for their work. At the same time, they have developed techniques of their own for obtaining data about the meanings that have been given to words by the speakers of a language.

Semantics is related to lexicography, but usually implies broader inquiries into the uses of language and the meanings of words. Whereas lexicographers tend to ask, "What does a word mean?" semanticists ask, "What do we mean by 'mean'?" For example, inquiries have been made into such questions as, What are the functions and varieties of definitions? What is the relationship between a word and its referent? What are the functions and varieties of statements? When can a statement be called "meaningful"?

Some linguists have tried to push themselves beyond such questions to even more difficult ones (and, some say, with predictably precarious results). For example, In what ways does language—its grammatical structure and lexicon—influence our nervous system? or, to put it another way, To what extent is our nervous system a product of language habits? Alfred

Korzybski preferred to place these questions under the heading *neurolinguistics*. Later, he used the term *general semantics*.

As we have already indicated, similar questions were asked by Whorf. By common but not unanimous consent, the terms *metalinguistics* and *psycholinguistics* have been used to designate inquiries of this type.

The work of I. A. Richards practically defies labeling. Although he was an early contributor to questions of semantics, probably his most important inquiries are those he made into the behavior of readers. For Richards, the question "What does a literary work mean?" tends to be misleading and unproductive. He substituted for it the question "How do readers make meanings when confronted by literary works?" From our point of view, there are no more exciting or relevant inquiries into language behavior than those conducted by Richards (and this bias will be confirmed in Part Two).

There remains for us to mention those studies conducted into the development of language in children, to which the chief contributor has probably been Jean Piaget. The *psychology of language* or *language development* is an appropriate designation for such inquiries.

The chart you will find in the back of the book will provide a visual overview of the subject matters that have been studied by linguists. Moreover, as we have also said, in Part Two of the book we discuss at some length the developments in several of the important fields mentioned here. Nonetheless, a few additional remarks need to be made now about the areas we have listed.

First, the subject matters of linguistics appear to be growing in quantity and complexity, as Sapir hoped they would. Ten years from now the areas under investigation by linguists may be twice as large as the number we have identified. Theoretically, there is no limit to the varieties of inquiries that can be made into the role of language in human affairs. As I. A. Richards observed, our libraries should be filled with works on the subject. And it is likely that they will be, although many kinds of inquiries must be postponed until there are adequate instruments with which to conduct them. There is nothing unusual in science about the proliferation of subject matters.

Below, for example, is a passage from an article by Marjorie Grene which explains what modern biologists are like:

> The difference between [the two fronts of biology] is illustrated by their different research procedures. In the laboratories of molecular biologists one can find blackboards full of calculations, expensive electronic equipment, carefully isolated preparations of various tissues of micro-organisms or metabolic substances; but anything that looks like a plant or an animal is conspicuously absent. True, molecular geneticists still perform breeding experiments, but for this purpose they usually use bacteria phage or other borderline organisms invisible to the naked eye. Even in electron microscopy, where techniques of looking, of "pure observation," are undoubtedly crucial, the structures "seen" are far removed from ordinary vision.
>
> Ethologists, on the contrary, must spend hour after hour and week after week devotedly *watching* animals—living animals—in laboratory conditions, in zoos, or best of all, in the wild, managing or submitting to environments which differ greatly from species to species. They do, of course, perform experiments of great ingenuity and sophistication, interfering with the environment of their subjects in such a way as to infer from altered or constant behavior the fundamental patterns of action which certain situations call forth. For example, they spend much time trying to discover whether a given pattern of action is "innate" or "learned." In every case, however, their concern is not with tissue cultures, proteins, or genes, but rather with the actions of whole, individual animals or groups of animals. However abstract and elaborate their theoretical explanations of such behavior may be, they always talk about *what animals do,* and this is a very different subject matter from that of their molecule-oriented colleagues. Indeed, the ethologist more nearly resembles his more old-fashioned colleague, the morphologist; both are engaged in the study of perceptible patterns in things that are visible and audible on the surface of our world.

In linguistics, the situation is somewhat similar. Just as there are biologists who appear to be physicists, or chemists, or mathematicians, or good old-fashioned zoologists, there are linguists who appear to be physicists, or mathematicians, or psychologists, or just good old-fashioned comparative philologists. All of which leads us to a second point about the areas of inquiry we have identified: If you feel that the fields we have marked off are not sufficiently exclusive or precise, bear in mind that the categories of research in science are often quite arbitrary and do not in practice lend themselves to precise demarcation. To refer again to the passage about biologists: The ethologist is hard to distinguish from the morphologist. The molecular biologist is hard to distinguish from the molecular geneticist. Similarly, in linguistics, the lexicographer may be hard to distinguish from the semanticist, the semanticist from the psycholinguist, the dialect geographer from the usage scholar, and so on.

Third, linguists in each of the fields we mentioned have tended to emphasize different activities of the scientific process. For example, those concerned with phonology have been particularly effective in developing their techniques of observation and a taxonomy for classifying data. Those working in the field of grammar, especially in recent years, have been most active in developing what they call a theory of grammar, and have paid less attention than their predecessors to description. Some linguists, like Korzybski and Whorf, and to some extent I. A. Richards, have contributed to the linguistic enterprise mainly by formulating suggestive hypotheses and lines of inquiry. Thus, in a certain sense, not all of these fields of inquiry are equally "scientific." Some areas are further along in the refinement of procedures than are other areas. Linguists working in phonology have developed their describing procedures to a far more precise and systematic degree, than, say, those working on problems of meaning. But having said this, we must hastily add that all linguistic inquirers assume that one of their important objectives is to improve their methods of investigation, and they all accept the general ground rules of science.

CHAPTER 3

What Is Linguistics Good For?

WE COME NOW to the questions which are the basic motivation for this book. Linguistics is here to stay. At an increasing (some say, a stampeding) pace, linguistics is influencing the teaching of English. To be modern, schools must claim to use "a linguistic approach" as well as the "new math," the "new science," and the "new social studies." But is linguistics useful for education? Can it help children to write more effectively? to read with greater comprehension? to speak better? to listen better? to think more critically? to conduct inquiries intelligently? These are the kinds of questions asked by teachers of English and by parents, most of whom feel that the value of linguistics must be judged by its capability to yield affirmative answers.

In raising these questions, we must make a few observations about their underlying assumption. Notice that the questions concern *behavioral changes.* What is being asked by all of these questions is, "How will students be different if they study linguistics?" From our point of view, this kind of question is entirely legitimate; in fact, it is the only kind of question worth asking about a new development in education (or for that matter, about an old practice). Our bias should be made clear at once: *If linguistics holds no promise for producing desirable changes in student behavior, then it ought to be dis-*

carded as a school subject. We stress this view because it has been asserted by some that the major reason for studying linguistics is that it is "good *in itself* to know," or that language, being the most humane of all the humane studies, should be taught because it is "good to know about it." Here is a particularly forthright expression of this point of view by Paul Roberts:

> But certainly we need to bother about the English language, as we need to bother about English literature, and for the same reason: that it is a good thing to know. We don't or shouldn't, study literature for practical reasons; we don't read *Othello* in order to ascertain the dangers of jealousy. Neither should we study language primarily to avoid the peril of the dangling modifier. We should study language, particularly our own language, just because it it is a good thing to know. Of all the humane studies, it is the most humane, since it is the thing that is central and common and peculiar to mankind. If we find that study of it has practical value–improves our spelling, eliminates our comma faults–so much the better. But whether it does or not, it deserves a prominent place in the curriculum and and particularly in what we might want still to call the composition class.

From our point of view, the argument above is in error on several grounds. To begin with, it reflects a wholly inadequate definition of "practical." One may not read *Othello* in order to ascertain the dangers of jealousy, but one does read *Othello* for entertainment or catharsis or aesthetic pleasure or for a dozen other entirely "practical" reasons. Some of these reasons may stem from social needs, or psychological needs, or even economic needs. But they always reflect the *purposive* nature of people. Similarly, while it is surely trivial to study language primarily to avoid such perils as the dangling modifier, language can be studied because it helps one to *be* something he is not, or *do* something he is unable to do, or *feel* something he would like to feel. No one (not even a paranoid schizophrenic) does anything for "its own sake." People do things because their activities amuse them or relieve them or inform them or enrich them or advance them or even demean them, each of which is an eminently practical purpose. When students are asked to do things in school, those who do the asking ought to have some behavioral objective in mind. When left unexplained, sentences like "It is a good thing to know" simply avoid the basic questions they are supposed to answer: In what sense "good?" "Good" for whom? For what human purpose? In what human context? In fact, an excellent reason for studying language is that it can help one to be wary of sentences like "It is good." As I. A. Richards observes in *Principles of Literary Criticism:*

> We are accustomed to say that a picture is beautiful, instead of saying that it causes an experience in us which is valuable in certain ways. The discovery that the remark, "This is beautiful," must be turned around and expanded in this way before it is anything but a mere noise signalling the fact that we approve of this picture, was a great and difficult achievement. Even today, such is the insidious power of grammatical forms, the belief that there is such a quality or attribute, namely Beauty, which attaches to the things we rightly call beautiful, is probably inevitable for all reflective persons at a certain stage of their mental development.

Of course, one might say that when language is referred to as a humane study there is the implication that those who study it will become, in some sense, more humane, more liberal of mind and spirit. If this is the claim, it is certainly worth considering most seriously, for there can be no more practical subject to study than that which will produce men of kind, prudent, tolerant, and liberal tendencies.

The problem here is, "How is this to be accomplished?" By telling people things that are good for them? By showing them how systematic certain linguists are? By holding oneself up as a model, and saying, "I have studied language. Behold how humane I am."? These are questions that have been left largely unanswered by those who link linguistics with humanism. Perhaps those linguists who are accustomed to saying things like "The study of language needs no justification. It is its own justification." are deceived by their own clichés. In any case, teachers cannot afford to be similarly deceived. Nor can they afford to be deceived by the facile assertion, frequently made, that the major contribution of linguistics is that it offers to English teachers a subject matter. In our single-minded view, we would again be forced to ask: A subject matter for what use? (Of no use, goes the answer; it's just good to know it.) In what sense "good?" (Good, because people ought to know it.) Why ought people to know it? (Because it's good.) This kind of reasoning will not get us anywhere; more important, it will not get teachers or students of English anywhere either.

We repeat: The questions raised at the beginning of this chapter about the uses of linguistics are in our view both legitimate and urgent. This is why we stressed early the importance of defining linguistics in a way that would permit it to achieve useful educational objectives. A definition that conceives of linguistics as a subject matter (and particularly, a subject matter about grammar) will eventually lead only to elaborate rationalizations in behalf of what Whitehead called "inert ideas"—ideas, as he put it, that are "merely received into the mind without being utilized, or tested, or thrown into fresh combination," but which are generally thought to be "good" for you anyhow.

What is needed is a definition of linguistics that transforms the subject into actions that result in improved language and learning behavior.

By "improved language and learning behavior," we mean improvements in the ways in which students *use* language (i.e., in reading, writing, speaking, listening), along with a knowledge of how to go about learning that which is yet to be learned. We believe linguistics can contribute importantly to these goals *when it is defined as the use of scientific processes of inquiry into the role of language in human affairs.*

LEARNING HOW TO LEARN (*Learning Behavior*)

What students most need to learn in schools is how to learn. This is the position taken by almost all modern educational philosophers, from John Dewey to Jerome Bruner. This is also the major emphasis in all of the new curricula—the new math, the new science, the new social studies. The emphasis is placed on the *how* of learning rather than the *what.* It has come to be recognized that the facts, definitions, and generalizations of a discipline—its content—are the *end products* of the learning process, and tend to have little meaning and durability from the student's point of view if the processes of inquiry which produced them are not understood. It is therefore asserted that the basic task in teaching is to help students to learn how inquiries are made. What is important is not that students be given answers—even the "right" answers—but that they learn how answers are produced, how knowledge is generated, how learning is conducted. As Jerome Bruner remarks in "Growth of Mind":

> There is nothing more central to a discipline than its way of thinking. There is nothing more important in its teaching than to provide the child the earliest opportunity to learn that way of thinking—the forms of connection, hopes, jokes, and frustrations that go with it. . . . At the very first breath, the young learner should be given the chance to solve problems, to conjecture, to quarrel as these are done at the heart of the discipline.

By assigning the highest priority to the *processes* of scholarly inquiry, this view places subject matter, or content, in its proper perspective. Most people recognize that the schools have traditionally regarded the accumulation of facts, even in the absence of a purposeful context, as a wholly worthwhile goal in itself. Accordingly, our educational methodology is largely designed to distribute facts as efficiently as is humanly (or mechanically) possible, with the result that our classrooms quite often assume something of the atmosphere of a rigged quiz show. The students are supplied with advance information, given a few days to memorize it, and are then required to feed it back when they are properly cued. It is an odd anti-intellectualism that says to a student: You do not need to know how knowledge is generated—what skills, attitudes, and methods are needed in order to produce knowledge. You only need memorize what others have already discovered through their inquiries. If you can learn to restate an arbitrarily determined portion of what they have said, you have done enough.

Such a philosophy produces a most insidious kind of waste of human potential, because the intellectual sterility it engenders is obscured behind grades on tests and percentages of students who pass or fail. Investigations of "retention of learning" of what is taught in this manner show again and again that within a short time such "learning" quickly disappears. Every teacher who conducts classes in this way has had the experience of loudly articulated student dismay at the prospect of being questioned during the second marking period about "knowledge acquired" during the first marking period. Such an attempt is regarded as grossly unjust, since all of the students (and most of the teachers) feel it unreasonable to expect anyone to recall anything "learned" in this way beyond the last quiz (given not really to determine what each student has learned, but what grades are to be assigned—and the relationship between the two is seldom as close as commonly assumed). "Fact obsolescence" is one of the most vivid signs of ours times. What are students to do with a random collection of obsolete facts? How do students learn to evaluate what they know? What have they been taught that will enable them to *ask* the questions that need to be asked? How will they continue to learn?

This point of view does not demean "subject matter." The making of definitions, the accumulation of facts, and the formulation of generalizations are indispensable phases of the inquiry process. Rather, this point of view asserts that it is not enough to know the "facts"—not when the facts change so quickly, not when the facts are merely "received into the mind without being utilized or tested . . . ," not when the facts reveal nothing of their origin. Ernest Nagel has expressed this view eloquently:

> . . . for a belief to be intelligently held, it is not sufficient that the belief happens to be true or claimed to be true by someone else. It it essential for a liberal intelligence that it know something of the nature of the grounds upon which the belief is maintained to be true.

By a "liberal intelligence," Nagel means the kind of mind that knows what to believe because it knows how beliefs come to be formulated. Linguistics can contribute toward the development of such a mind.

LEARNING TO USE LANGUAGE MORE EFFECTIVELY (*Language Behavior*)

This objective has been pursued so vigorously for so long by so many people that its meaning would seem to require little explication from us. What is meant by "effectively," however, is worth some elaboration.

In this context, the word *effectively* denotes a good deal more than the more conventional word *correctly* ever did. The notion of "correctness" in relation to language is quaintly naive, more appropriate to a class in etiquette for the *nouveau riche* than to persons concerned with human communication. The word *effective* is intended to reflect a plainly pragmatic concern with language as an instrument of human survival. The inquiry approach to language study is not primarily concerned with the "cosmetic" dimensions of usage. Simply put, evaluations of various possible language choices and decisions (among various possible "usages," for example) are based largely on the criterion of whether or not they accomplished their purpose.

Function, then, determines form. By observing real language in real contexts in this critical manner, certain basic generalizations about how language form affects language function can be identified inductively by anyone who talks. In this way, not only are traditional purposes of language instruction accomplished, but students also confront, and learn to deal with quite consciously, such concepts as *relativity* and *contingency,* along with that of *function* as a primary determinant of form.

Most of the stages of inquiry that we identified in the first chapter involve special ways of using language. Indeed, learning how to learn—in conventional academic terms, at least—means learning how to use verbal symbols. One needs to do certain things with language in the defining process, in the question-asking process, in the classifying process, in the generalizing process, and so on. Thus, education in how inquiries are made is, in large measure, education in using language. Moreover, this suggests that any teacher—regardless of the subject he or she is teaching—is, or should be, a language teacher. This is so not only because the inquiry process is largely a language operation, but also because *all subjects in the school curriculum are language.* Allow us to explain briefly.

There is an old story about a mother who was boasting to a neighbor of her son's academic achievements. At one point, the mother called her son into the room and insisted that he demonstrate his brilliance at once. "Harold," she demanded confidently, "say something in geometry for Mrs. Green."

The point of the story is supposed to be that the mother succeeded in demonstrating not her son's brilliance but her own ignorance. After all, who can "say" anything in geometry? Of course, if Harold were as brilliant as his mother believed, he *could* "say something" in geometry. For example: "Equals added to equals are equal." He could also say something in physics, biology, chemistry, history, geography, and any other subject in the school curriculum.

What we call a "subject" consists of "concepts" and "structures" that are codified in symbols, and almost exclusively in verbal symbols at that. (Mathematics is the most obvious exception to this.) Nothing is anything until we call it something; then it "is" whatever we call it. This is not a metaphysical position; it is merely a description of how we operate. A "concept" or a "structure" turns out to be "bits" of the process-world around us arbitrarily selected from a universe of possibilities and named, ordered, and related. If we do not do this with any portion of whatever it is that is around us, then, for all human purposes "it" doesn't exist. On the other hand, if we do have a name for "something," chances are we will see "it" whether "it" is there or not. Creating the symbols by which we codify our perceptions of something or other is one stage in the process of generating a subject. Beyond the names of the "bits" themselves is the process of *ordering* (placing in some sequence) and *relating* (patterning the sequence) the bits. The extent of the process of ordering and relating is, of course, determined by the limits of the symbol system within which this is done. So it turns out that a "subject" is "simply" a way of talking about some rather arbitrarily selected portion of the process-world about us.

All of this means that in an educational program that aims at helping students to use language better, the students would have to study the various "languages" people use to express their knowledge of and feelings about themselves and the world. How are these "languages" similar? How are they different? Is the language of a fairy tale different from the language of a scientific report? Is one language "better" than the other? How would you judge? Is the language of a newspaper story different from the language we call a short story? Is there a particular way of using language when you are stating facts? Is there a different way when you are expressing an opinion? What is a fact? What is an opinion? Is there a language about language?

The question arises, How can students answer such questions? and here we come to the second point we must make:

The only lasting way to make students better users of language is to help them become good *observers* of how language works. This, after all, is the first step in our becoming good at anything. First, of course, we must be interested in becoming "expert" in whatever it is—in this case, language. Then, if we solicit assistance from an expert we find that he is instructing us in how to observe differences that make a difference. Expertise, we all know, consists mainly in being able to observe differences that the non-expert fails to note. "It's all the same to me," says the novice. In other words, the process of becoming a master of any human skill, on any level of behavior, consists essentially of being able first to observe and then to act on differences that make a difference. The most sophisticated kind of expert is one who knows which differences to ignore —which differences do not make any difference. This ability is what produces the impression of "ease" in any expert performance; no energy is wasted on the irrelevant. For such reasons as these, then, the first step in training students to become more expert users of language is to refine their abilities at observing real language in actual use, with particular attention to differences that make a difference.

"My son is coming to do without me," wrote Emerson in his *Journal,* "and I am coming to do without Plato." There are only two kinds of English teachers who can say, "My students are coming to do without me." The first kind has been "turned off" by students who find their work in English dull and irrelevant. The second kind has helped students to become such astute observers of language that they can make their own evaluations of how well language is being used. S. I. Hayakawa has described the basic orientation of such teachers:

> Among present-day teachers of English—at least those who have been trained in modern linguistic science—it is believed that accurate knowledge of the facts of current usage in different social classes, on different social occasions, among different occupational groups, and in different areas of the country, and knowledge of the processes of linguistic change are essential if one is to develop in his students the ability to write and to speak well. The emphasis in instruction is not upon authoritarian rules and principles, but upon the development of curiosity and habits of accurate observation of language-in-process, whether in the writings of Dickens, at Chamber of Commerce meetings, or in labor-organizing drives. Styles of discourse, whether in scientific papers or in under-world argot are studied, and their effectiveness within their social context is noted. Such training in linguistic observation

> produces students, who, instead of being petrified into inarticulateness by stilted notions of "correctness," take delight in the variety and richness of the English language, and seek to cultivate that flexibility of linguistic resources that will enable them to take in stride whatever problems of communication they may encounter.—"Semantics, Law, and Priestly-Minded Men," *ETC.*, XIX, No. 3 (October, 1962).

Here, then, is the problem, focused at last: How can linguistics develop the habits of accurate observation, of curiosity about how language works? How can linguistics develop flexibility and resourcefulness in using language? How can linguistics develop the attitudes that foster growth? For answers, we are led to a consideration of the kind of classroom that Hayakawa describes.

INDUCTIVE OR DISCOVERY METHODS OF TEACHING

Of all the popular misconceptions that are given daily support in our schools, perhaps the most quietly destructive is the notion that science is something that is studied only in science courses. Like the belief that art is something found only in museums, this is a rather modern heresy, certainly never dreamed of by the founders of the Royal Society. Nevertheless, it is perfectly apparent that when contemporary educators speak of science, what they mean is the "hard sciences"—physics, biology, chemistry, and so on—and in particular the facts which each science claims are within its province. This prejudice, which is reflected in both our curriculum design and our teaching methodology, has created the strong impression among students that "science" is specific and technical information that one learns in certain designated courses in the curriculum; in short, that science is an isolated and specialized activity that has application only to limited areas of human experience.

Of course, we have stressed throughout this book the opposite view—that science is a process, a way of knowing, of confirming, and of continuing to learn. We have also stressed that linguistic science is this process applied to the study of language. We come, then, to the conclusion that the major educational significance of linguistics *is not in its new terminology or results, but in its methods of inquiry or discovery.* If this point is missed, then almost all the potency of linguistics for changing student behavior is lost. This is why linguistics so often is—and must be—linked to what is called inductive, or discovery, methods of teaching.

Various other names have been given to this kind of teaching. Jerome Bruner, who has had so much to do with advancing its cause, uses the term "hypothetical mode" (of teaching), as distinct from the "expository mode," which he equates with "traditional teaching." Jerome Kagan refers to the "method of inferential learning." Others have used the term "inquiry training." Still others have used the terms "inductive" and "discovery," the latter being preferable, we think, because (1) it is the most widely known, and (2) its connotations are the least restrictive.

What is the discovery method of teaching and learning? It is, first of all, a prescription of the roles that teacher and students must play in the classroom. Specifically, it requires that the burden of intellectual inquiry be carried by the student, not the teacher or textbook. In the case of the English class, it requires that the students try to solve problems not unlike those that linguists must solve. In other words, it requires that students become involved in processes of defining, question asking, data gathering, observing, classifying, generalizing, and verifying in matters of language. It implies that the students play an important role in determining what lines of inquiry are worth pursuing and a pre-eminent role in determining what arguments and conclusions are worth embracing.

In addition to conventional functions, such as evaluating student achievement, the function of the teacher is twofold: First, to insure that students will engage seriously in processes of inquiry by immersing them in an atmosphere of relevance; second, to guide the inquiries that the students make. Of course, there are hundreds of questions that can be asked—

indeed, have been asked—concerning the refinements and particulars of discovery methods. How much structure must the teacher provide? How many varieties of discovery methods are there? What arrangements for communication among students should be made? At what points should the teacher provide some sort of "closure" to a problem? To what extent should the teacher allow "wrong answers" or unproductive procedures to go unchecked? Is it reasonable to expect any "new" knowledge to emerge from student inquiries? What kind of of personality must the teacher have in order to create such a classroom environment? How much "subject matter" will be amassed? Will it be remembered? And so on. There are useful answers that can be given to some of these questions. Research in the years ahead will provide still more answers (as well as more questions). What it is essential to remember is that in the "discovery" English class, the student is *trying to behave as language scholars do.* The grammarian, the semanticist, the lexicographer, the language historian, the dialectologist, the language sociologist are what they are because of what they do. What *do* they do? In brief, they try to solve problems about language by adopting certain attitudes and using certain procedures. To the extent that students in school emulate them, they are *doing* lingusitics.

That is the message. Here are some commentaries:

The discovery method of teaching is indifferent to specific doctrines. Its emphasis is on *how* students do their thinking, not on the indoctrination of particular thoughts.

All too frequently, other methods of teaching tend to motivate the student to emulate the teacher, not to free himself of the teacher. John Dewey describes this behavior extremely well:

> The operation of the teacher's own mental habits tends . . . to make the child a student of the teacher's peculiarities rather than of the subjects he is supposed to study. His chief concern is to accommodate himself to what the teacher expects of him, rather than to devote himself energetically to the problems of subject matter. "Is this

right?" comes to mean "Will this answer satisfy the teacher?"—instead of meaning "Does it satisfy the inherent conditions of the problem?"—*How We Think* (Boston: D. C. Heath and Co., 1933).

Methods of teaching that stress "the facts," and set up the teacher or textbook as the sole and indisputable authority on the "Truth" of facts, do not prepare the student for life in a world where he must choose in some meaningful way between conflicting bodies of "fact" and conflicting versions of the "Truth" given by different "authorities."

It must be emphasized here that the subject matter of linguistics offers no protection against dogmatic and authoritarian teaching. In fact, one of the most depressing developments in the teaching of English is the tendency of some teachers who have accepted the results and terminologies of linguistics to teach the new judgments in the same authoritarian manner in which they previously taught the old ones. Instead of telling their students that a sentence is a group of words expressing a complete thought, they now tell them that it is a structure made up of form classes. Instead of telling their students that "It is me" is wrong, they who fancy themselves liberals now tell their students that it is right.

Such teachers have misunderstood the fundamental relationship between scientific procedures and learning. For so long as students are neither equipped nor encouraged to reflect on the truth or falsity of these statements, so long as they remain strangers to the basis of conviction or belief, any definition or linguistic description will be a matter of indifference or resentment to a clearheaded student.

The inductive method of teaching, by stressing the procedure of inquiry—methods of evaluating as well as of gathering facts—attempts to develop in the student a critical attitude toward authority and its pronouncements. The dangers of authoritarianism in the classroom have been clearly stated by Bertrand Russell:

> Passive acceptance of the teacher's wisdom is easy to most boys and girls. It involves no effort of independent

> thought, and seems rational because the teacher knows more than his pupils. . . . Yet, the habit of passive acceptance is a disastrous one in later life. It causes men to seek a leader, and to accept as a leader whoever is established in that position. It makes the power . . . by which plain men are misled into accepting old systems which are harmful to the nation and to themselves.—"Education," in *Selected Papers of Bertrand Russell* (New York: The Modern Library, Inc., 1927), p. 106.

Discovery methods assume that the methods of teaching we use carry the burden of our efforts to teach attitudes. "Perhaps the greatest of pedagogical fallacies," wrote Dewey, "is the notion that a person learns only what he is studying at the time. Collateral learning in the way of formation of enduring attitudes . . . may be and often is much more important than the spelling lesson or lesson in geography or history." When a youngster is *doing* linguistics in a "discovery" classroom he is acquiring the attitudes of scientific inquiry because he must use them in his everyday work in school.

It remains for us to comment here that, like linguistics itself, discovery methods of teaching are relatively new in the schools. No one can say with certainty what the ultimate outcomes will be. Education is always an adventure, and the best one can do is to suggest programs and procedures that have high goals and that hold the promise of success.

PART TWO

INTRODUCING PART TWO

PART TWO includes descriptions of the significant work done by linguists in a particular field, and of programs and procedures employed in selected schools. The reader will note that there are relatively few illustrations drawn from elementary-school classrooms. This fact reflects not a lack of "discovery" activities in the elementary grades, but the limitations of the authors' research at that level. In general, however, elementary-school teachers have reported little difficulty in adapting the procedures and materials in Part Two to their classrooms.

In any case, all the examples given are specifically intended to foster the development of those "habits of mind" described by John W. Gardner as being necessary to our survival:

> If we indoctrinate the young person in an elaborate set of fixed beliefs, we are ensuring his early obsolescence. The alternative is to develop skills, attitudes and habits of mind and the kinds of knowledge and understanding that will be the instruments of continuous change and growth on the part of the young person. Then we will have fashioned *a system that provides for its own continuous renewal.*
>
> This suggests a standard in terms of which we may judge the effectiveness of all education—and so judged, much education today is monumentally ineffective. All too often we are giving our young people cut flowers when we should be teaching them to grow their own plants. We are

stuffing their heads with the products of earlier innovation rather than teaching them to innovate. We think of the mind as a storehouse to be filled when we should be thinking of it as an instrument to be used. . . .

We are moving away from teaching things that readily become outmoded, and toward things that will have the greatest long-term effect on the young person's capacity to understand and perform. Increasing emphasis is being given to instruction in methods of analysis and modes of attack on problems. . . . In all subjects it means teaching habits of mind that will be useful in new situations—curiosity, open-mindedness, objectivity, respect for evidence and the capacity to think critically.—*Self-Renewal: The Individual and the Innovative Society*

CHAPTER 4

Grammar

GRAMMAR AND THE LINGUISTS

IN DISCUSSING the subject of grammar with dozens of parents, scores of teachers, and hundreds of students, we have been astonished to discover that most of them do not have the slightest idea of where a grammar comes from. Even worse, most people seem unaware that grammars—that is, descriptions of the structure of a language—are invented and written by human beings. They seem to believe that a grammar is something that is just *there,* like the seasons, or the tides, or the stars. Such people are predictably confused by "modern developments" in grammar, since they cannot imagine "modern developments" in the seasons, the tides, or the stars. For this reason, we feel it important to begin with a modest historical review of grammar. We trust that this beginning will not be unduly burdensome, but it will help us to make clear that grammars, like literatures, are only the products of men, living at a particular time and place, expressing their particular biases, wisdom, and foolishness.

Prior to 1700 there were few books written on the subject of the structure of English. One notable exception was Ben Jonson's *English Grammar* (published in 1640), which was among the first books on the subject that did not proceed under the assumption that the term *grammar* necessarily implied the study of Latin grammar. (It is perhaps relevant to note here that the term "grammar school" was originally used to designate a school in which the study of Latin grammar was given prominence.) A typical attitude toward grammar in the seventeenth century was that expressed by Jonson's contemporary, William Shakespeare, who, as a schoolboy, had probably been required to read William Lyly's *Latin Grammar.* (In 1542, Henry VIII made it the standard text for schools.) Perhaps in revenge for the grammatical persecution he suffered, Shakespeare wrote (in *Henry VI, Part II*):

> "Thou hast most traitorously corrupted the youth of the realm in creating a grammar school. . . . It will be proved to thy face that thou hast men about thee that usually talk of a noun and a verb, and such abominable words as no Christian ear can endure to hear" (IV, vii).

In any case, the Elizabethan age was one of creative and rewarding experiment with language and, particularly, of prodigious growth in vocabulary. Shakespeare and his contemporaries were far less concerned with analyzing the English language than with using it, adding to it, and exploiting its possibilities. The eighteenth century, however, was quite different. In the first half of that century fifty grammar books were published, and in the latter half more than two hundred. There are at least two clearly established reasons for this impressive interest in grammar.

Eighteenth-century Englishmen were fond of calling their age the Augustan age, a name chosen because of a neoclassicist admiration for the culture of Rome under Emperor Augustus. This point has some significance, because the first, although lesser, reason for the eighteenth century's concern for grammar was that Englishmen had rediscovered the golden ages of Greece and Rome. When the educated eighteenth-century Englishman compared his language with the language of Cicero and Virgil, he was saddened, if not appalled. Although Bacon's *Novum Organum* (published in 1620) was one of the last great works written in Latin, literary England remained extremely partial to that language. John Dryden, in fact, was so partial to Latin that he did not think that English had a grammar of its own.

In order to validate the grammatical propriety of what he wrote, he translated his words into Latin to make necessary "corrections." As a result of this somewhat quaint practice, Dryden discovered, as did others addicted to the same procedure, that it was awkward to conclude an English sentence with a preposition, since it did violence to Latin when translated. This grammatical "rule" and others (e.g., it is incorrect to split English infinitives, presumably because it can't be done in Latin) form part of the grammatical inheritance willed to us by eighteenth-century writers.

But something else was at work in eighteenth-century England of even more importance than a rediscovery of the virtues of Rome. In about the middle of the century a reorganization of the social and economic structure of England began to take place, as machine and power tools replaced ancient hand tools. England began its Industrial Revolution.

As men left their farms and headed for the cities, and as an agricultural society increasingly became an industrial society, England found itself with a new class of people—a "middle class," people who were no longer chained to the land, but who, on the other hand, were neither intellectually nor socially prepared to lead the cultivated life. In their desire to attain a status to which they felt their new-found affluence and freedom entitled them, these people assumed an almost compulsive interest in English grammar. To them, language became a medium of social prestige, or, to use a modern term, a medium of upward social mobility. Toward this end, wealthy merchants and their wives employed tutors to inform them of the elegant modes of speech. The tutors responded to the demand by producing "latinized" English-grammar books, which is to say, books attempting to describe the structure of English in terms of the structure of Latin. One of the most influential writers of this period was Oxford scholar Robert Lowth, later Bishop of London, whose *Short Introduction to English Grammar* was published in 1762. In 1795, Lindley Murray, an American, wrote a grammar that enjoyed enormous popularity. (More than a million copies were sold from 1795 to 1850.) The problems faced by these teacher-grammarians (many of whom were clergymen or philosophers) in trying to construct a grammatical frame for English were formidable. The following statement by Karl Dykema is a fair account of the difficulties encountered by these "fathers of English grammar":

> First, [the 18th-century grammarian] was faced with the mass of material that a total living language with all its dialects presents, though of course he did not recognize that he had this problem. Second, he was totally unprepared to make an original and independent analysis of any language because he had never been confronted with the problem of analyzing a language for which no formal description existed; that is, he had no acquaintance with a methodology of linguistic analysis. Third, he was fatally handicapped by an intimate acquaintance with the concepts of classical grammar, concepts which had come to be accepted as universals, though many of them had little relevancy to English. . . . Fourth, the cultural atmosphere in which he worked tended to make him look upon English as an inferior or at best a defective language. . . . Fifth, he found himself in a position never enjoyed by his classical predecessors, the position of enjoying a large audience, made up principally of members of the middle class who had social aspirations. This last point is of tremendous importance because it explains how formal English grammar got itself so firmly established in the schools. For we must not forget that especially during the past century and a half a very important function of the schools has been felt to be that they should help the ambitious to push their way socially upward into a class where control of a particular variety of English was an important means of admission.

One other thing might be said for the eighteenth-century grammarian. He was honest. He stated quite frankly that he did not like the language as it was and had written his grammar to improve it. Jonathan Swift, for example, proposed that the English establish an academy similar to the ones that existed in Spain and France, in order to prevent the language from further "decay." This was also Sam Johnson's intention when he set about to produce his comprehensive English dictionary, published in 1755. (Johnson was wiser than most, however, in that he ultimately acknowledged the impossibility of halting linguistic change.) Perhaps the most typical expression of the eighteenth-century view of grammar is to be found in Thomas Sheridan's *General Dictionary of the English Language* (1780). Sheridan wrote:

> . . . so little regard has been paid to the [English language] that out of our most numerous array of authors, very few can be selected who write with accuracy . . . nay it has lately been proved by a learned prelate in an essay upon grammar, that some of our most celebrated writers, and such as have hitherto passed for our English classics, have been guilty of great solecisms, inaccuracies, and even grammatical improprieties, in many places of their most finished works.

In short, it was typical of the grammarians of the eighteenth century to assume (1) that language was a divine inspiration, originally perfect, but debased by man; (2) that, consequently, language possessed a natural logic that could not be violated even by common consent; which is to say, common usage; (3) that the consummate expression of linguistic purity and perfection was to be found in Latin and Greek, especially Latin, and that the grammar and inherent logic of Latin were criteria by which the excellence or depravity of any language could be judged; (4) that English could be improved by the application of rules of Latin and by the insistence on a strict adherence to these rules; and (5) that the function of a grammarian is to preserve, protect, and otherwise defend the language from "decay."

Beginning in the nineteenth century and then, particularly, in this century the assumptions and results of "traditional" grammarians were sharply criticized by linguists (first, historical linguists, such as Otto Jesperson; then descriptive linguists, such as Leonard Bloomfield). More recently, "generative" or "transformational" grammarians have come to the defense of traditional grammar in ways that we will discuss later. But the major criticisms, which are three, still stand.

First, the notions of such grammarians as Lowth, Sheridan, and Murray were almost classically unscientific, which is to say that their assertions were not consistently based on careful observation of the language they were attempting to describe. Second, their methods of analysis and classification were unsystematic and inconsistent. And, third, they failed to distinguish between objective inquiry and personal preference. Some examples of each of these failures follow:

Failure to observe. The Latin language is classified as an *inflected language.* This means that the principle device by which to express grammatical relationships is a system of word-endings, or, more accurately, changes in the forms of the words themselves. Thus, the word *amorem* is, by its very form, a noun; the word *amare,* a verb. Modern English relies to some extent on inflections to indicate certain grammatical concepts, e.g., the *-ed* verb-ending, which signals past tense, and the *-s* noun-ending, which signals plurality. But unlike Latin and Old English (which had thirteen possible inflectional endings for the various classes of nouns) the *principal grammatical device of Modern English is word order; that is, the position of a word in a syntactic structure.* Thus, the word *love* does not assume a specific grammatical meaning until it appears in some relation to other words. For example, it functions as a noun in "*love* is a many-splendored thing," a verb in "I *love* you," and a modifier in "she had a *love* affair."

Had eighteenth-century grammarians been concerned with accurately describing the structure of English, it is unlikely that they would have missed this point. But, as indicated before, their classical bias led them to the false assumption that all languages could be described in terms of the grammatical devices of Latin, and thus prevented them from making this easily observed distinction between Latin and English grammar. As Charlton Laird said in *The Miracle of Language:*

> The root fact of English grammar is that English words have precise meaning in a certain position, and are gibberish in another position. This fact, however one wishes to phrase it, embodies the most important grammatical truth that can be enunciated about English: *Order in the*

> *sentence is the basis of English grammar*. And yet, barring a few students of Modern English, the chances are that not one in a hundred readers of this page will ever have heard anything like this statement before. That is the simple, the almost unbelievable truth.

One need only add that the general ignorance of this truth can be attributed to two factors: (1) the unwillingness or the technical inability of the eighteenth-century grammarians to observe with objectivity the English language, and (2) the failure of the schools to disassociate themselves from the eighteenth-century tradition.

Failure to be consistent and systematic. The traditional definition of a noun is that it is a word that names a person, place, or thing. Obviously, a great many nouns either do not fit this description at all or require the most fanciful stretching of the imagination to do so. For example, the words *explosion* and *stimulation* (and in fact most nouns with the *-ion* ending: expulsion, admonition, anticipation, expectation, etc.) do not name a person, place, or thing, but rather an action or state of mind. In any case, it is quite a subjective matter to decide what phenomenon a word names. The confusion to which such a definition leads is comparable to that which would follow from defining an airplane as "a vehicle people use when they are in a hurry." Perhaps most people who use airplanes are in a hurry (although many obviously aren't), but this is not the way one tells the difference between an airplane and other means of transportation. In short, while the traditional definition of a noun is a definition of sorts, it is clearly neither exclusive enough nor objective enough to be wholly serviceable. The same is true of the traditional definition of a pronoun ("a word used in place of a noun"). If one were actually to *use* this definition, the following sentence would contain three pronouns (instead of the one it actually contains):

> Although Notre Dame receives national recognition for its fine football teams, the University demands high standards of scholarship from athletes wishing to play for "the Fighting Irish."

Of course, pronouns are often used in place of nouns (e.g., *its* is used in place of *Notre Dame's*), but so are other nouns and phrases (e.g., *University* and *"the Fighting Irish")*, thus rendering the definition partially irrelevant.

What is even more confounding than a lack of distinctiveness in the definitions of English "parts of speech" is that they possess no consistent base. Nouns and verbs are defined by their "meaning." Adverbs, adjectives, conjunctions, prepositions, and pronouns are defined by their "function" (e.g., "an adjective is a word that modifies a noun"). Interjections are sometimes defined by their "form," but there is no general agreement as to how this "part of speech" is to be handled. For example, from *The Century Collegiate Handbook:* "An interjection is a word *thrown into* speech to express emotion. It has no grammatical connection with other words." This would seem to be a definition based partly on meaning, partly on form, and partly on function, although what the precise meaning of the term "thrown into" may be is clearly open to question.

The absence of a systematic classification of "parts of speech," although confusing, is no more so than the traditional method of identifying sentences. A sentence is customarily defined as a group of words expressing a complete thought. Such a definition reveals pitifully little, since what constitutes a complete thought—the key to the definition—is left unexplained. Are the following utterances complete thoughts? "No taxation without representation"—"Wherever particular people congregate" —"Roosevelt was President"—"Fifty-four forty or fight." Probably only "Roosevelt was President" would be regarded by teachers as a sentence, although from many points of view it is far from being a complete thought. For example, wouldn't one at least need to indicate which Roosevelt one is talking about before being satisfied that the thought is complete?

The major difficulty in the method of analysis used by eighteenth-century grammarians is that the method relies heavily on the most subjective element in language, meaning; and meaning is almost always a matter of individual interpretation. This leads to the same kind of muddle that would result in botany if plants were classified by their beauty or lack of it.

Failure to distinguish between description and prescription.

Most of us find it either tragic or amusing that Galileo's colleagues refused to look through his telescope for fear of seeing things that might violate their cherished conception of the universe. We take it for granted that an astronomer's principal task is to report what he observes, unencumbered by personal prejudices. If he wishes to remold the universe to conform to some personal image of beauty or truth, he may do so, but usually in the capacity of a poet or philosopher, never as a scientist. As we have said, modern linguists try to confine themselves to descriptive statements about language, and to avoid expressions of personal bias. Compare this attitude with that expressed by Lord Chesterfield in his review of Sam Johnson's dictionary:

> The time for discrimination seems to be now come. Toleration, adoption, and naturalization, have run their lengths. Good order and authority are now necessary. But where shall we find them, and at the same time, the obedience due to them? We must have recourse to the old Roman expedient in times of confusion, and choose a dictator. Upon this principle, I give my vote to Mr. Johnson to fill that great and arduous post. And I hereby declare, that I make a total surrender of all my rights and privileges in the English language, as a free born British subject, to the said Mr. Johnson, during the term of his dictatorship. Nay, more, I will not only obey him like an old Roman, as my dictator, but, like a modern Roman, I will implicitly believe in him as my Pope, and hold him to be infallible while in the chair.

Guided by their own predilections of the way the language ought to be used, Mr. Johnson and others made numerous ex cathedra statements about English, which, while interesting and often learned, did not always have very much to do with the way the language was actually used. A mathematician named Johannis Wallis, for example, feeling that the language would be improved if a distinction were made between the uses of *shall* and *will,* invented the famous "rule" which is now fully incorporated in our grammatical tradition.

The point is that eighteenth-century grammarians were *pre-*

scriptive in their approach to language, in the same way that theologians are prescriptive in their approach to morality. There is, of course, nothing wrong with prescribing ways of human behavior so long as one is clear about the motives for doing so. But prescription is not a substitute for *description,* and when one fails to distinguish between them, there is inevitable confusion.

Beginning in the late nineteenth century, and largely through the work of men who were interested in studying the history of languages and in comparing one language with another, the study of language began to lose its haphazard and prescriptive orientation and to assume a more scientific basis. Comparative and historical philologists accumulated an enormous amount of information about the English language and began to develop a standardized method of classifying their data. Such scholars as Jacob Grimm and Karl Verner were able to discover a certain regularity in linguistic change, particularly in the changes of consonant sounds. Alexander (Sharpe) Ellis and Henry Sweet (the phonetician who, it is said, was the model for Shaw's Henry Higgins in *Pygmalion*) did massive analyses of the sound system of English.

In 1894, *The Outline and Structure of English,* by the Danish scholar Otto Jespersen, was published. It was one of the first books on English to be based on a careful observation of the structure of the language, with particular reference to the changes that had taken place in its structure. Jespersen declared that change in language is inevitable; he considered it improvement rather than corruption. (Today, linguists are by no means in agreement on this point; most will say only that linguistic change is inevitable.) Jespersen also demonstrated how English had been altered, not corrupted, by loan words from other languages and by the elimination of many of its inflectional forms. In 1924, in his *The Philosophy of Grammar,* he proposed a new system of English grammar in which he advanced the notion that, among other things, English has only two tenses (present and past), not six; all other alleged "tenses" being in reality aspects of time represented by the composition of phrases (have gone, will go, shall have been taken, etc.).

This phase of linguistic scholarship is usually thought of as "historical grammar," to distinguish it from what it replaced, traditional grammar. It can be profitably thought of as the beginning of descriptive linguistics, as the two quotes that follow suggest. The first is from Henry Sweet's *New English Grammar,* published in 1891. The second is from H. C. Wyld's *Elementary Lessons in Modern English Grammar* (1925). Both reflect a point of view that would have been incomprehensible to Bishop Lowth and Lindley Murray, but which was taken for granted by Sapir, Bloomfield, and other twentieth-century linguists.

> In considering the use of grammar as a corrective of what are called "ungrammatical" expressions, it must be borne in mind that the rules of grammar have no value except as statements of facts: whatever is in general use in a language is for that very reason grammatically correct.

> A grammar book does not attempt to teach people how they ought to speak, but on the contrary, unless it is a very bad or a very old work, it merely states how, as a matter of fact, certain people do speak at the time at which it was written.

Beginning in this century, the principles, assumptions, and procedures of what is called *descriptive linguistics* were developed. What were these linguists trying to do? In the first place, they not only redefined the term *grammar,* they also redefined the function of grammarians. As the second quote (Wyld) implies, the grammarian was stripped of his historic prerogative to make value statements. He confined himself to description rather than prescription, and his definition of grammar was stated in nonevaluative terms. For example, a representative definition of grammar is: *Grammar is the study of the ways in which a language achieves structural sense.*

Note that this definition makes no mention of "good grammar" or "bad grammar." To the descriptive grammarian, "he don't have none" is as grammatical as "he doesn't have any." Both structures convey meaning; as a consequence, one is as interesting and informative to the grammarian as the other. The study of those structures that are preferred by one social group or another became known as the study of *usage.* Usage studies (notably one conducted by Sterling A. Leonard in 1932, *Current English Usage*) have been extremely rewarding in adding to our fund of knowledge of the English language. (For example, the Leonard study informs us that "I wish that I was rich," "None of my friends live here any longer," and "I felt badly about it" are commonly used by those who speak the "standard" dialect.) But inquiries into usage were not to be confused with inquiries into structural devices. As one linguist put it: "Usage is to grammar as etiquette is to behavior. Behavior simply notes what people do; etiquette sets a stamp of approval or disapproval upon actions, or sets up standards to guide actions." In other words, a second accomplishment of descriptive grammarians was to make important distinctions among the different aspects and problems of language study. Moreover, descriptive grammarians devoted much energy to devising objective and consistent classification systems and to making explicit their major assumptions.

One of the most important assumptions that the descriptive linguist makes is that the spoken language *is* the language. No human community has ever been found that did not possess a speech system fully developed for the purposes of its users, although many have been found that have no writing system. (The fact is that there are more languages in existence that have no writing system than languages that do.) In making this assumption, the linguist is not underestimating the importance of writing to the culture of a people. He is simply acknowledging the fact that speech is the primary symbolization of reality, and that writing (especially an alphabetic or phonetic system of writing) is an attempt to represent the sound system of a language. Thus, in investigating a language, a linguist is, at first, concerned with identifying the various sounds that the speakers of that language habitually use.

Owing largely to the brilliant work of George Trager and Henry Lee Smith, Jr., as well as that of Kenneth Pike, a rigorous method of linguistic analysis came widely into use. The system segmented language into layers of structure—with phonology first, morphology next, syntax last.

Phonemics. The attempt to identify and classify all the sounds used in a given language is known as *phonetics.* But obviously, one does not need to know *all* the sounds of a language in order to analyze it, since most of these sounds have such a slight variation that even the speakers of the language are not aware of any differences. For example, it can be demonstrated on an oscillograph that no person can say the same word twice in identical ways. And yet the fact that one cannot say the word *person* exactly the same way as one said it before does not cause one's listener any difficulty in recognizing both utterances as, for all practical purposes, the same word. The linguist therefore tries to identify the smallest unit of sound that makes a functional difference in the meaning of words. The method that linguists use to determine the *phonemes* of a language is to contrast words that are identical in every sound except one, then to determine if the meanings of the two words are the same or different. For example, the words *pill* and *bill* are identical in every respect except the initial consonant sound. A linguist would conclude from this (since these words mean different things) that *p* and *b* are separate phonemes in the English language. This is further demonstrated by the difference in meaning between *rapid* and *rabid.* For other phonemic differences contrast *thy* and *thigh, bit* and *bet, team* and *time, Confucian* and *confusion, place* and *plays.*

It is generally acknowledged that the English language has approximately forty phonemes. The range among all languages is somewhere between twenty-five and sixty. Included in the concept of phoneme are differences in meaning that are expressed through such devices as *stress* (contrast the noun *con'tract* with the verb *contract'*), *pitch* (contrast "What's that on the road ahead?" with "What's that on the road, a head?"), and *juncture* (contrast *nitrate* with *night rate*).

Morphemics. After identifying the phonemes of a language, the linguist proceeds to the next layer of the sound structure of a language, which is the identification of words, or, technically speaking, *morphemes.* A morpheme is distinguished from a phoneme by the fact that a morpheme, by itself, has meaning whereas a phoneme, by itself, does not. Thus, the phoneme *p* carries with it no particular meaning, but when combined with the phoneme *i,* the sound that results (*pie*) does have meaning. Morphemes are only crudely correlated with that less precise term, words. They may also be likened to what are commonly called prefixes, suffixes, and infixes. (Contrast *unusual* with *usual* and it will be obvious that *un* has a meaning.) Morphemes, then, are of two kinds: *free* (those that have meaning by themselves, e.g., *pie*) and *bound* (those that take on meaning only when attached to other morphemes, e.g., *un*). Languages can be classified according to the ways in which they employ their morphemes. For example, *analytic* languages use few bound forms, *synthetic* (or inflected) languages use many.

Syntax. Moving on from this point, the linguist proceeds to investigate the manner in which morphemes are arranged into meaningful phrases, clauses, and sentences. This layer of structure is commonly called the *syntax* of a language. The descriptive linguist makes a distinction between two kinds of meaning that operate in language. The first kind, *lexical* meaning, may be defined as those objects, events, processes, and so on, in the world around us to which our verbal symbols refer. Thus, each of the following words has a lexical (or dictionary) meaning: love, little, happy, boy, mother. But as they are arranged here, this group of words has no meaning beyond the lexical meaning of each individual word. They will remain in this "meaningless" condition until we provide them with some kind of structural sense, or *structural meaning.* By structural meaning linguists mean such ideas as case, tense, number, and so forth. These ideas express the relationships that exist among lexical symbols. Thus, if we say, "A little boy loved a happy mother," we have told you who did the loving and who was loved (*case*), who was little and who was happy (*modification*), and something about the time of the event (*tense*). You will notice that this was largely accomplished by arranging the words in a particular order.

From the standpoint of descriptive linguistics, the most widely known and influential study of the structure of English sentences is that conducted by Charles Carpenter Fries (notably in his *The Structure of English,* 1954). Fries not only devised a structurally based system for identifying "parts of speech" but also attempted to describe the structural components of that unit of speech which we call a sentence. Fries defined grammar as the study of the linguistic forms that "signal" structural meaning. He identified five major devices by which structural (or grammatical) meanings are expressed in English:

1. *Word order:*
The sequence in which words and word groups are arranged.

2. *Function words:*
Words similar in function to those words that are commonly called "auxiliary verbs," "prepositions," and "articles." They are largely devoid of lexical meaning, their main function being to indicate relationships among the meaningful words with which they appear. Thus, to use Professor Fries' famous example, "ship sails today" is ambiguous until one supplies the utterance with a function word (sometimes called a structure word). "The ship sails today" means one thing; "ship the sails today" means quite another.

3. *Inflections:*
Alterations in the forms of the words themselves to signal changes in meaning and relationship.

4. *Derivational contrasts:*
These are word endings that are similar to inflections in that they alter a grammatical idea by their presence. But they are unlike inflections in that they are permanent forms. Some examples of these contrasts (prefixes and suffixes) are: amuse*ment,* black*en,* beauti*fy,* beauti*ful,* beauti*fully, en*force, *a*sleep.

5. *Intonation:*
The system of stress, pitch, and juncture that would, for example, help one to distinguish the two possible meanings of "She gave her dog biscuits."

Some languages rely to a very great extent on morphological "signals" to express grammatical relationships, but Modern English, as has been said before, depends principally on syntactical "signals." Thus, where at one time the case signal of English nouns could be found in the words themselves, this signaling device is entirely absent from Modern English. The only way to learn the case of an English noun today is to observe its relationship to other words in a sentence. Pronouns, of course, still retain morphological signals: *I* becomes *me, he* becomes *him*. And yet, so complete is Modern English's reliance on word order that when the two signals conflict, most English-speaking people will trust word order rather than inflection. Here is an example: "Me and him loves Mary." When asked what this sentence means (specifically, Who does the loving and who is loved?), most Americans will respond by saying that he and I are doing the loving and Mary is the one who is being loved. This is said in spite of the fact that there are three morphological signals that would indicate the opposite to be true! (The verb agrees in form with Mary, and *him* and *me* are in the objective case.)

Fries and others also identified what they called the basic sentence patterns of English, and tried to describe the ways in which such sentences can be expanded into complicated structures. For example, the structure *Birds eat worms* (N-V-N) is taken as a "basic sentence pattern" because it is "a minimum free utterance"—that is, not part of any larger structure. (For the same reason, "Hello" is defined as a sentence.) W. Nelson Francis, in *The Structure of American English,* showed how such basic structures can be expanded: (*a*) Through "modification": *Large birds eat worms.* (*b*) Through "coordination": *Large birds eat worms and fish.* (*c*) Through "predication and complementation": *That large birds eat worms and fish is well known.*

There remains, for our purposes, to remark that the emergence of descriptive linguistics was met with vigorous and largely intemperate objections by some important members of the intellectual community. Jacques Barzun accused Charles Fries of engineering the "demise of grammar in the American schools." Others of less distinction charged that the results of descriptive grammar would lead to a breakdown in communication, in morals, and in the social order. On a few occasions, the controversy was reminiscent of the struggle, almost a century earlier, between Darwinists and their theological opponents. To give Darwin's antagonists their due, *On the Origin of Species* threatened a five-thousand-year-old theology. The work of Bloomfield, Sapir, Trager, Smith, and Fries merely challenged a 200-year-old school tradition.

Attacks from uninformed laymen—columnists, college deans, movie critics—eventually subsided, and descriptive grammar moved to the edge of orthodoxy. At that point, "transformational," or "generative," grammar emerged, and a new school of grammarians challenged "the Establishment."

Generative grammar received its most prominent expression in 1957 with the publication of Noam Chomsky's *Syntactic Structures* (although Zellig Harris' work, in a similar direction, preceded Chomsky's by several years). There has formed around Chomsky a group of dedicated "transformationalists," including Robert Lees, Owen Thomas, Paul Postal, Jerrold Katz, and Morris Halle, who have shown little reverence for the work of their immediate predecessors. However, before discussing the basic assumptions of generative grammar, we must point out that generative grammarians accept *most* of the basic assumptions of the structural linguists. For example, both groups make a careful distinction between speech and writing. Both insist on rigorous and objective analysis. Both work hard at clarity of definition. Both sharply distinguish descriptive from prescriptive statements.

The major difference between descriptive grammarians and generative grammarians is in the ways in which they define grammar (which leads them, of course, to ask different kinds of questions).

To the generative grammarian, grammar is defined as a set of ordered rules that characterize the infinite set of grammatical descriptions of its sentences. The structuralist, it is claimed, is satisfied to *describe* the different kinds of sentences people utter, and to identify the structural characteristics of those sentences. In this way, he believes he is describing the grammar of a language. Not so, says the generative grammarian. The job of the grammarian is not merely to describe the sentences produced by speakers of a language, but also to *explain* how such sentences are produced. After all, the structuralist can never describe *all* the sentences spoken, since their number is infinite. What is needed is a theory of grammar—an abstract set of statements (i.e., rules)—which explains how an infinite number of sentences can be produced from a limited number of basic structures. Generative grammar begins, then, with the identification of a limited list of "kernel sentences"—somewhat equivalent to the "basic sentence patterns" of the structuralist. All sentences that are not kernel sentences are defined as "transforms"—that is, variations, expansions, extensions, or permutations of kernel sentences. The major task of the grammarian, in generative approaches, is to state the rules by which "kernels" generate all the possible sentences of a language. For example, the explanation, known to every traditional grammarian, of how "the boy hit the ball" (active voice) can be transformed into "the ball was hit by the boy" is an illustration of the kind of rule sought by generative grammarians. The difference is that in most cases the traditional grammarian merely felt intuitively that there is a connection among certain sentences. The generative grammarian tries to make explicit the basis of this intuition by stating rigorous rules and formulas that explain these "connections." It must be noted here that generative grammarians seem to have considerable respect for the work of traditional grammarians, admiring in particular the intuitions of and questions asked by the latter. In fact, one linguist has defined generative grammar as rigorous, systematic, and explicit traditional grammar.

We can be almost certain that transformational grammar is not the last word on the subject. There is every reason to believe that the future will provide new grammars and new theories of grammar. As W. Nelson Francis has written, "It is possible that the most important contribution of the middle 20th century to the study of grammar will be to pluralize it. We find ourselves studying not grammar, but grammars." Undoubtedly, this is exciting news for grammarians. What does it mean—what has it meant—for students in the English classroom?

GRAMMAR IN THE SCHOOLS

The teaching of grammar used to be both dull and uncomplicated. In fact, it probably was dull because it was uncomplicated. This is not to suggest that the grammar that students were asked to learn was always clear or accurate or useful. It is to suggest that regardless of the limitations of traditional grammar, it was the only grammar to teach. At the moment, there are no fewer than three grammars: traditional, structural, and generative. The future holds the promise of still more.

What is the English teacher to do in the face of this development?

Before considering this question, we must make a few important observations about what has happened in the schools with grammar in the past.

As teachers of language and, incidentally, as teachers of language teachers, we have often pondered this question: Which is more distressing, the fact that most people find the study of grammar confusing or the fact that most people find it boring? The answer to that question, although not a trivial one, is not nearly so suggestive as the question itself, for it happens to be a fact that more time is spent in our schools, from the seventh to twelfth grades, on teaching grammar than on any other single phase of English instruction. If the observations underlying our question are valid, this means that teachers of English spend more time in confusing and boring their students than in doing anything else. Of course, English teachers are not any more insensitive to their students than are other kinds of teachers; most of them are perfectly aware that grammar is neither their students' best loved nor best comprehended subject. They tend, therefore, to justify what they are doing by advancing the notion that grammar is "good" for their students. In claiming this, they are echoing a belief that has been held for so long that it has become part of the folklore of education. A list of the most prominent claims made in behalf of the study of grammar over the years would include these: that it (1) disciplines the mind, (2) aids in the study of foreign languages, (3) helps one to use better English, (4) helps one to read better, and (5) aids in the interpretation of literature.

What does research tell us about these claims?

Among the earliest inquiries into the efficacy of teaching grammar was one made by Franklin S. Hoyt, the results of which were published in the *Teachers College Record* in November, 1906. After subjecting to a series of tests the assumption that "the study of grammar disciplines the mind," Professor Hoyt concluded that "the position seems reasonable that the study of formal grammar as ordinarily pursued below the eighth grade, being ill adapted to immature pupils, will tend to retard the natural development of the child, rather than further 'training in thought' and the disciplining of the understanding."

In 1913, a study by T. H. Briggs substantiated Hoyt's findings. In 1923, William Ascher conducted an inquiry into the relationship between a knowledge of grammar and writing ability. He capsulated his findings in the following words: "We may, therefore, be justified in the conclusion that time spent upon formal grammar in the elementary school is wasted so far as the majority of students is concerned."

In 1932 and 1933, N. C. Holtman and E. Frogner, respectively, published studies that indicated there was no connection between the study of grammar and improved language usage and sentence structure. Additional studies were conducted in 1941, 1942, and 1945. The results continued to be negative. In 1948, Fred G. Walcott, in an article entitled "The Limitations of Grammar," wrote: "Within the subject of English . . . certain illusions have persisted for nearly half a century despite a good body of research to disprove them. One of these illusions is the supposed efficacy of grammar in improving oral and written composition and in preparing pupils for college."

The 1950 edition of the *Encyclopedia of Educational Research* summarizes the results of most of these studies. We believe the following excerpts from the *Encyclopedia* are worth reading:

> [*On disciplining the mind*]: Experimentation in this area failed to yield any significant evidence supporting the belief in grammar as a disciplinary subject.
>
> [*On the interpretation of literature*]: The results from tests in grammar, composition, and literary interpretation led to the conclusion that there was little or no relationship between grammar and composition and grammar and literary interpretation.
>
> [*On improved writing and usage*]: Further evidence supplementing the early studies indicated that training in formal grammar did not transfer to any significant extent to writing or to recognizing correct English. In general the experimental evidence revealed a discouraging lack of relationship between grammatical knowledge and the better utilization of expressional skills. Recently, grammar has been held to contribute to the better understanding of the sentence. Yet, even here, there is a discouraging lack of relationship between sentence sense and grammatical knowledge of subjects and predicates.
>
> [*On the study of foreign languages*]: In spite of the fact that the contribution of the knowledge of English grammar to achievement in foreign languages has been its chief justification in the past, the experimental evidence does not support this conclusion.
>
> [*On the improvement of reading*]: The study of grammar has been justified because of its possible contribution to reading skills, but the evidence does not support this conclusion.
>
> [*On improved language behavior in general*]: No more relation exists between knowledge of grammar and the application of the knowledge in a functional language situa-

tion than exists between any two totally different and unrelated subjects.

> [*On diagraming sentences*]: The use of sentence diagraming as a method of developing sentence mastery and control over certain mechanical skills closely related to the sentence has been subjected to a series of experimental investigations. In general the studies indicate that diagraming is a skill which, while responsive to instruction, has very slight value in itself. There is no point in training the pupil to diagram sentences except for the improvement it brings in his ability to create effective sentences. The evidence shows that this is insignificant.

If we accept these studies as valid, we must ask ourselves: What goes on here? For surely the meaning of these studies is that rarely have so many teachers spent so much time with so many children to accomplish so little.

Several points need to be made about this dismal record. First, in all cases cited above, traditional grammar was being taught, not descriptive or generative grammar. Second, more recent, although scanty, research suggests that structural linguistics does *not* come any closer than traditional grammar to achieving the goals usually set for grammar instruction. Third, although there is little research on the effects of generative grammar we feel safe in predicting that *if generative grammar is taught in conventional ways it will be found to be as useless as any other system of grammar.*

Many generative grammarians sense this themselves, which is why they have so often insisted that grammar must not be taught with the expectation that it will produce desirable changes in student behavior. For example, Robert Lees, writing on "The Promise of the Transformational Grammar" in *The English Journal,* remarks: "If English grammar is to be taught at all in the secondary schools, then there is little if any justification for teaching it in conjunction with rhetoric or literature; rather, such a study of language belongs in the area of science and general education along with psychology and anthropology."

Other generative grammarians have taken the view, as we have indicated, that English grammar should be taught as part of the English curriculum because "it is a good thing to know," which translates into "I get enjoyment from doing this particular work, and I think students will enjoy it too." One can only hope that such grammarians know more about grammar than they do about children. One extremely honest grammarian has recently admitted in a book on linguistics and grammar that he has been *"fascinated" by sentence diagramming since the seventh grade!*

Let us look briefly at the kinds of sentence diagrams which, some feel, it is "good for students to know." FIGURE 1 is an

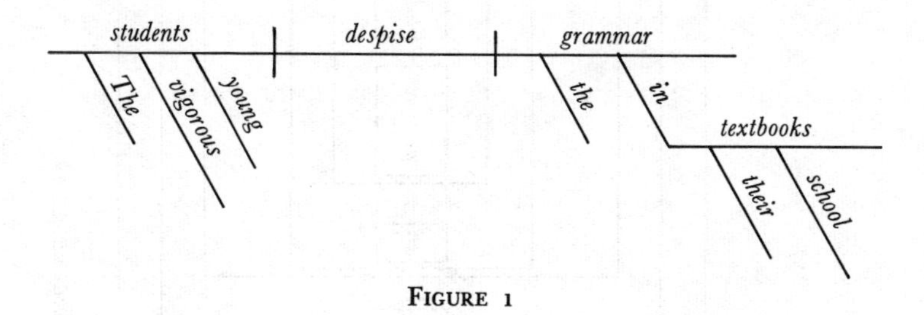

FIGURE 1

example of a sentence diagram based on the familiar system introduced by Alonzo Reed and Brainerd Kellog sixty years ago.

FIGURE 2 is a diagram based on the principle of immediate constituent analysis, used widely by structural linguists. This system divides all parts of a sentence into "two's," continuing until all elements have been paired in some way.

FIGURE 3a and 3b represents recent "advances" in grammar, since it does not simply break down a sentence into its component parts, but attempts to show how a certain kind of sentence can be generated, in this case, passive sentences. It must be stressed that this diagram (more accurately called a derivation) is an abbreviated version.

Now, what does all of this mean? First, we would submit that only an extremely naive person would suppose that children can learn to write better English by doing such diagrams. In this, we are saying nothing unusual, since both the available

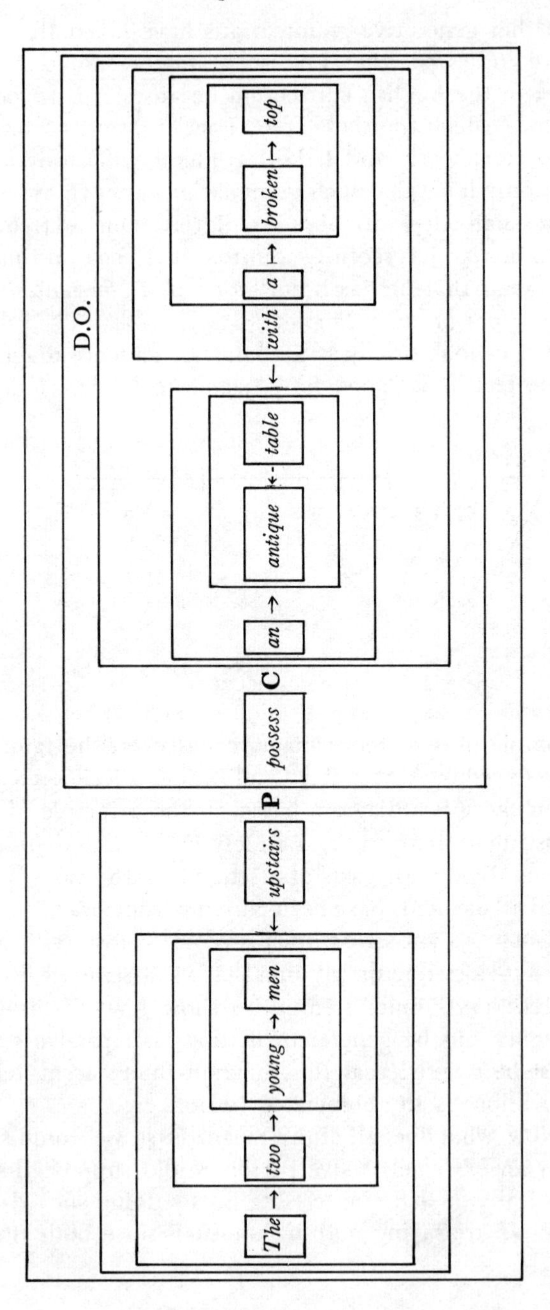
D.O.
The
two
young
men
upstairs
P
possess
C
an
antique
table
with
a
broken
top

FIGURE 2

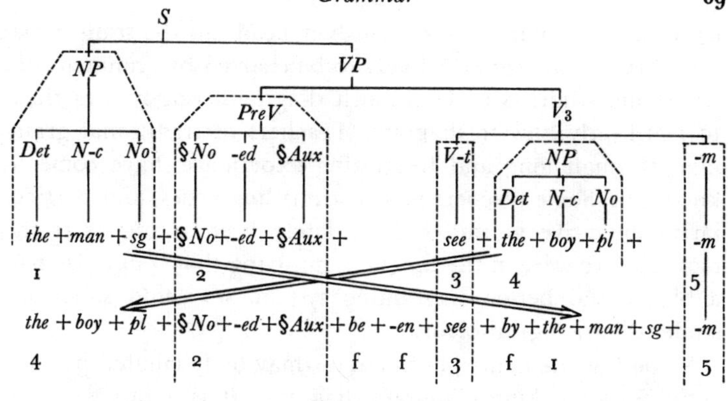

FIGURE 3a

Then T2 must be applied to bring about the subject-predicate agreement:

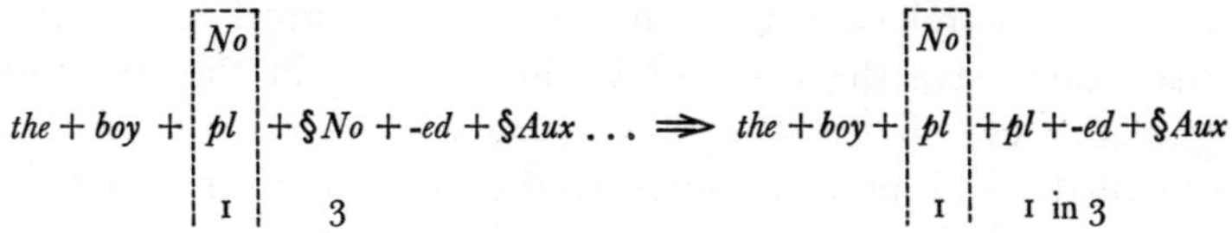

the + *boy* + *No* *pl* + §*No* + -*ed* + §*Aux* . . . ⇒ *the* + *boy* + *No* *pl* + *pl* + -*ed* + §*Aux*

1 3 1 1 in 3

FIGURE 3b

With proper application of M-rules and a further T-rule which removes the §*Aux*, this becomes: *The boys were seen by the man.* If T1 were not applied, T2 and the proper M-rules would give the sentence the form: *The man saw the boys.* These two sentences are agnate; the rule T1 is a formal generative statement of the relation between them.

research and most grammarians themselves tell us the same thing. One obvious reason is that by the age of eight, physiologically normal children already *know* the essential structure of their language. If they did not, they would be unable to talk. To put it in terms of the structuralist, children know (i.e., they use) the word order of their language; they know its devices of modification, subordination, coordination, and so on. To put it in terms of the transformationalist, children know the "rules" by which "the boy is tall" is transformed into "the boy is taller than I." In fact, by the age of eight, children already have stored in their heads all the transformational rules that are ever likely to be charted by grammarians. By asking students to learn such diagrams, one invites them to learn only how to diagram. Teachers of traditional grammar, through long and frustrating experience, have come to know this. Some teachers of structural linguistics, and particularly generative grammar, have lately been acting as if the main failure were in the *diagram,* implying that if only we had a bigger and better diagraming system, we could solve our students' writing problems.

Second, while many grammarians may be fascinated by such activities as making elaborate diagrams, it is a rare seventh-grader who will find any enjoyment in it whatsoever. The same is true of eighth-, ninth-, tenth-, eleventh-, and twelfth-graders.

Third, because such activities are not enjoyable, are not perceived as relevant, and, in any case, are largely rote exercises, they have the effect of stifling interest in the study of grammar, even in the study of language.

Fourth, and most important, the particular grammatical system (including the technical manipulations associated with it) used in a classroom is *not* the decisive variable in making grammar study both interesting and useful. Some of the dullest, most irrelevant, and generally useless grammar teaching goes on under the banners of "structural linguistics" and "generative grammar." The decisive factor, as we have stressed, is the *method* by which learning is conducted. In this, again we say nothing unusual. Plato said it. Cicero said it. John Dewey said it. Jerome Bruner has been saying it. And G. Robert Carlsen, former president of the National Council of Teachers of English, has also said it:

> We all know that a minor revolution has taken place in the teaching of sciences and mathematics in American schools. Those of us in English suddenly find ourselves faced with a desperate need to catch up. But our attempts to imitate the revolutions in science and math have been based on inadequate understanding of the changes in those fields. While these two areas have changed their content to some extent, they have changed their methodology to a

> greater extent. The mathematicians and scientists saw clearly that the way a student studies in the subject is fundamental if he is to learn to think within the subject. In English most of our efforts have been in the area of content to be taught. It is time that methods of teaching English again become a major concern within our profession. . . . Methods can usually be described as a choice of one of three roles the teacher selects for himself and his students. . . . Role 1: The Teacher Tells—The Student Memorizes and Stores . . . Role II: The Teacher Molds—The Student Conforms . . . Role III: The Teacher Stimulates—The Student Teaches Himself. . . . Plato defines the teacher as an "intellectual midwife.". . . My feeling is strong that English at present is structured to use *telling* and *molding* about 95 percent of the time. We have not really learned as yet how to set up situations in which our students are stimulated and permitted to make discoveries on their own. . . . Inquiry and discovery are the very essence of the reading of literature, yet here too, we as teachers have substituted didacticism and molding.

We come back, then, to the original question: What is the English teacher to do in the face of the developments in grammar? How can he avoid the sterility of grammar teaching? How can he use grammar to advance intelligence? Stated below are descriptions of specific procedures, strategies, and problems that have been used and are being used by English teachers who have tried to answer these questions by following the suggestions implicit in Carlsen's point of view.

Some teachers have responded to the challenge of linguistics by raising for their students such questions as these: Why do we need a grammar? What assumptions underlie a grammar? What role does definition play in a grammar? What standards can be used as a basis for evaluating a grammar? In raising such questions, teachers are focusing at least as much on the "problems of grammar" as they are on the facts of any particular grammar. What they would like students to learn about grammar is, accordingly, different from what the traditional teacher wants his students to learn. The traditional teacher requires of his students obedience in learning one set of facts, one set of definitions, and one set of attitudes. Whether partial to Lindley Murray, Charles Fries, or Noam Chomsky, he views grammar as a closed system in which there are flaws, to be sure, but to which there are no alternatives. The inductively oriented teacher views grammars as simply another opportunity for students to learn something about the processes of inquiry into the nature of language.

One such teacher used, as the basis of a series of lessons, the following suggestion made by I. A. Richards (in the chapter "What Is Grammar?" in *Interpretation in Teaching*):

> The natural curiosity about how language works . . . struggles hard before it chokes. Formal descriptive grammar generates a resentment against the grammarian, which is traditional in the subject. I believe that this resentment can be made use of, and that it would be excellent pedagogy to open a course on the theory of grammar with an exhibition of some of the odd arbitrarinesses and mistakes of grammarians—to serve as a sort of animated cocoanut-shy for our pupils. To offer some of these absurdities for criticism, early, relieves the resentment, and to ask about them, "What on earth has been happening here?" sometimes opens a path into the subject which leads towards its very centre. The terminologies with which professional grammarians make such magnificent play had perhaps best be left out, or introduced only for picturesque effect. Amateur spectators need not be expected to wield such weapons.

The teacher provided his students (tenth-graders) with several different definitions of a sentence, taken from examples given in Fries' *The Structure of English*. His basic questions were, as Richards urged: What goes on here? Why the differences? He also provided several different "defenses" of the function of a grammarian. His questions were: In what ways do these men differ? Why would anyone want to do what these men propose to do? Which of the "functions" seems most useful to you? Why?

This teacher was concerned, with Richards, to minimize resentment against grammar, and to help foster *attitudes toward language study which encourage the student to continue learning.* This is a notion that cannot be emphasized enough. The most important learning that can occur is the development of attitudes that create an interest in learning.

The teacher was also interested in helping students see that knowledge and concepts are continually changing, even in grammatical studies. He hoped that this awareness would initiate *a sense of curiosity* about the subject. Perhaps the single most important idea behind this approach (and all the examples that follow) is that the teacher is taking the learner into account. What is emerging here is not a new subject matter but a new focus of attention: *the way students learn.*

It is quite common to hear English teachers refer to some students in the following terms: "They just don't want to learn." "They just aren't interested." "They just don't have the I.Q." "They just don't have the verbal ability." "They don't learn it no matter how many times I teach it."

Notice that the onus is always on the student. *What is it* that they do not want to learn? *What is it* that they are not interested in? How can something be "taught" if no one learns it? Why has there been so much discussion of the "structure of the subject matter?" Why so little about the "structure of the learner"? We have no less than Plato to remind us that ". . . education can accomplish its goal only if reason has an adequate emotional base." The adequacy of such an emotional base must be judged from student response—his interest, the degree to which his curiosity is aroused, the extent to which he engages his mind. The teacher, in this case, was working toward such goals.

Since one of the major tasks of any grammarian is to provide useful definitions and distinctive categories of grammatical phenomena, junior-high-school teachers in dozens of school systems throughout the country begin inquiries into grammar by having their students study the process of classification itself. For example, one teacher in Washington, D.C., provided her seventh-grade students with the following list of words:

fowl, carrots, apples, oranges, steak, meat, vegetables, chicken, hamburger, plums, bacon, pheasant. The students' problem was to arrange these words into a convenient system of classification. Another teacher, on Long Island, exhibited to her class thirty photographs of various sizes, shapes, colors, and subject matter. The problem her students had to solve was to devise a classification system for the pictures that would be both unambiguous and logical. The purpose of such activities as these is to help students to see that just as there are different ways of classifying foods and photographs, there are also different ways of usefully classifying words, phrases, and sentences, and to understand that any grammarian is faced with a similar problem.

The next step in this procedure is to have students go through the process of determining the various bases on which a grammar may be constructed. It is possible, of course, to devise a classification system based on the lexical meaning of words. (There is a class of words that name persons, places, or things.) But it is also possible to base a classification system on the physical forms of words. (There is a class of words that can be inflected for plurality and possession.) It is possible to base a system on the positions of words in a sentence. (There is a class of words that will fit in the blank space: "The ______ is good.") There are, of course, other ways of classifying words, and teachers have reported that when students are allowed to work on this kind of problem, they are often ingenious in discovering interesting criteria to use as a basis for a grammatical classification system.

With the kind permission of Alan Shapiro, chairman of the English Department, Isaac Young Junior High School, New Rochelle, N.Y., we have reproduced here one of his lesson plans from a series of lessons dealing with problems of definition in grammar:

Problems of Definition: What Is an Adjective?

The main purpose of the lesson will be to develop some understanding of the problems one faces in defining grammatical terms. The lesson will attempt to help students see that a definition of a term reflects the point of view of the definer, that definitions of grammatical terms may be approached in a variety of ways, and that no single type of definition is likely to be completely satisfactory.

Before this lesson the students will have been made aware of the fact that one commonly offered definition of an adjective is that it is a word which describes or which modifies a noun. We shall begin the lesson by examining the following sentences (which will be on the board, along with a chart of the following type) and the underlined words in them to see how well this definition holds up when it is examined closely:

1. The boy *smiled.*
2. Those men are *violinists.*
3. The boy is *crying.*
4. He became a *book* salesman.
5. Samoa is an *American* possession.

ADJECTIVES OR CLASS 3 WORDS

Defining by meaning	*Defining by function*	*Defining by form*	*Defining by position*
Adjectives describe	Adjectives modify nouns		

Questions: Strictly in terms of our definition of an adjective (a word which describes or which modifies a noun), are these words adjectives? Why or why not? If we call all of these words adjectives, are we making a statement which contradicts our earlier classification of any of these words? Why or why not?

This discussion should elicit the idea that we have, on previous occasions and in terms of other definitions, classified *crying,* for example, as a verb and *violinist* as a noun. Apparently, other types of words describe, and other types of words modify nouns.

Another possible approach to the definition of adjectives might be through the forms of such words. The students will be asked to suggest words which might fit the blank in the following sentence:

She is a _________ person than Kathy. (to be written on the board along with words suggested by students)

Questions: What do you notice about all of these words?

Why do all of these words end in *er*?

Can we now define an adjective as a word to which *er* may be added?

Consider the underlined words in the following sentences:

She is a famous person.
It was a rainy day.
He did a poor job. (to be written on the board)
Bob played a marvelous game.
She made a silly mistake.

Questions: Do all of the underlined words describe?

Do all of the underlined words modify a noun?

Can *er* be added to all of the underlined words?

When we define in terms of whether or not a word describes, what type of definition are we using?

In terms of whether or not a word modifies a noun?
In terms of whether or not *er* may be added to a word?
What conclusions can we draw about each of these different types of definitions?

What other possible types of definitions might help us to understand what an adjective is?

Assignment: Try to state a definition of an adjective in terms of pattern or position by substituting words in the following frames.

He is _____________. A ______ boy is ______.
He is very __________. He became __________.

Come to class prepared to state whether or not adjectives and only adjectives will fit in all of these frames or if not in all of them, in one or more of them.

It must be stressed that when students are engaged in such processes, they invariably learn a great deal about the structure of language because the structure of language is the data they must use in solving their classification problems. Some high-school teachers have challenged their students to compare and contrast the definitions and classification system of different grammars. One teacher in St. Louis asked her students to develop a chart in which such grammatical concepts as a phrase and a sentence were defined from as many different points of view as possible. The students in her class knew something about both traditional and structural grammar, and used, as a beginning, the definitions of these grammars. Eventually, they expanded their chart to include definitions that were either from some other grammatical system or not a part of any existing grammatical system. Below is a reproduction of the chart dealing with the concept of a sentence that the students developed:

DEFINING A SENTENCE

By describing its clause content:

1. A simple sentence contains one independent clause.
2. A compound sentence contains two or more independent clauses.
3. A complex sentence contains one independent clause and one or more dependent clauses.

By describing its patterns:

1. Noun Verb (1 2)
2. Noun Verb Noun (1 2 1)
3. Noun Linking Verb Noun (1 2L 1)
4. Noun Linking Verb Adjective (1 2L 3)
5. Verb Noun (2 1)

By stating its purpose or purposes:

1. A sentence makes a statement.
2. A sentence asks a question.
3. A sentence gives a command.
4. A sentence shows strong feeling.

By describing the way it is punctuated:

1. A sentence begins with a capital letter and ends with a period.
2. A sentence begins with a capital letter and ends with a question mark.
3. A sentence begins with a capital letter and ends with an exclamation point.
4. A sentence begins with a capital letter and ends with a semi-colon.

The students spent several weeks working on their chart and in the process learned several important things. They learned that grammars differ because grammarians define in different ways. They learned that there may be more than one answer to a single question. They learned, as Edward Sapir pointed out, that all grammars leak. They learned a great deal about the processes of defining itself. They learned something about how grammarians do their work and the problems they face. And, finally, they learned a great deal about phrases and sentences, since it is axiomatic that we understand something better when we look at it from more than one point of view.

It may be unrealistic to expect most teachers to involve their students in what some people call "comparative grammar." But even those teachers who wish to confine their students' work in grammar to one grammar have been able to proceed inductively. In other words, if the teacher regards structural linguistics as the best available grammar, he still has many opportunities to arrange his classroom so that his students can go through processes of analysis similar to those of the structural linguist. *Patterns of English,* by Paul Roberts, and *Discovering Your Language,* by Postman, Morine, and Morine, consist of carefully arranged problems, based on the structuralist's perception of what is important in language. These problems challenge students to analyze language in the manner of the structural grammarian (i.e., by discovering facts about the forms and syntactic positions of words). It is essential to note that in these books there are very few definitions, generalizations, or facts given to the student. Those that are given are tentative and serve only to define a particular line of inquiry. The entire thrust of the books is to require students to get at the facts, to formulate definitions, and to arrive at generalizations.

An even better approach was used by James Sabol in Shoreline High School, Seattle. Sabol was not in the least overwhelmed by the existence of different approaches to grammar. His concern was with promoting the intelligence of his students, not with the formulations of professional grammarians. Here is his report:

> What to do? Isn't the answer obvious? Let us return to direct observation, to direct experience, in a word, to reality. At a time when those of us in the trenches are torn among the structural grammarians, the transformationalists, and a nagging loyalty to the traditionalists; among Fries and Chomsky and Roberts; among morphemes and determiners and objective complements; what better time to begin a direct look at language?
>
> This year three sophomore classes at Shoreline High School began such an examination. These students are the same ones who asked the embarrassing questions. Congratulated for their perception and somewhat in the spirit of idol-destroyers, they were invited "really" to look at language. They began not with a text, not with what someone says about language, but with language itself. *They* spoke, *they* recorded, and *they* examined. Their purpose was to discover how real people really speak and write English, with what variations in effectiveness, and if possible, to learn what accounted for the variations. They were asked to begin their examination with no assumptions, no foregone conclusions.

Step one was for someone to speak a sentence. Step two was to record the sentence so that it might be examined. Step three was, at the suggestion of the teacher, to probe the sample for the answers to five fundamental questions:

1. Are all words alike?
2. Since obviously not, what are the kinds? (Orwell's "Principles of Newspeak" reminded the students of one kind of difference. Students freely discussed other differences from the number of letters in a word to rhyming possibilities. At the teacher's suggestion the students examined the words for differences of function.)
3. What are the differences of function?
4. Where do words occur in relation to each other by function?
5. In what patterns do words occur?

In the three weeks it took to answer these questions, two ground rules were in effect. There was to be no "outside" help; all examples and suggestions were to proceed from direct observation and discussion among the students of the three classes. At first a difficulty arose from those students who had learned their previous lessons the best, those with preconceived notions of such concepts as "noun-ness," "verb-ness."

The actual process of discovery may be described as uttering or listening to real sentences, recording them, suggesting answers to the questions, arguing, seeking advice, arguing again, forming tentative theories, and synthesizing. If that sounds sedate, the process in reality was wildly eager fifteen-year-olds tearing around the campus barking examples, monitoring friends' conversation at lunch, and hotly defending the "right" answers.

At the end of the study, results were published by and for the three classes. The answers turned out to be these:

1. All words are *not* alike.
2. Our language operates with four basic types of words:
   a. Labels—Sam, rock, pencil
   Substitutes for labels—it, someone, we

b. Predicates
that show doing—swim, hunt, sing
that show being—is, will have been, used to be

c. Pointers
that point to labels—big, new, pretty
that point to predicates—nicely, soon, yesterday
that point to other pointers—very, quite, overly

d. Connectors
that connect phrases to words—in, to, under, near
that connect clauses to words—unless, whenever, that
that connect, phrases, clauses, or words to each other—and, or, however, either

3. Pointers exist in three sizes: single word, phrase, and clause. They may be located in a variety of places resulting in considerable shift in emphasis.

a. A pointer that points to a label typically precedes it if one-word size (*raw* potatoes) or after it if phrase or clause size (potatoes *from Idaho,* potatoes *that are raw*), but exceptions occur (She likes her potatoes *fried.*).

b. Pointers that point to predicates may be placed with considerable latitude regardless of size (*Quickly* she hid the purse. She *quickly* hid the purse. She hid the purse *quickly.*).

c. Pointers that point to other pointers usually are placed before the modified pointer (a *very* warm day).

4. There is a discoverable pattern of words in English. "Control" words (subject, predicate, object, or complement) are the least variable. Pointers are extremely variable in size and location. The slight variability of control words and the endless variability of pointers make a discussion of patterns academic because the generative possibilities of any pattern are astronomically large.

The study produced welcome observations which the students had not anticipated:

1. English words function in a variety of ways.

2. One simply cannot describe the function of an English word until he hears it in a sentence.

3. Pointers are critical in English sentences. Most of an English sentence is comprised of pointers. What is left after the pointers are removed from an English sentence are a few control words and very little meaning. (Most *Shoreline* boys think that *green* socks look *pretty bad with blue shirts.*)

4. Language *is* related to composition. The style, the effectiveness, the cadence of English sentences may largely be explained in terms of variant locations of pointers. While I do not think that language study need be justified other than by the insights it yields into the essential nature of language—least of all by composition or usage—the students were encouraged, still in a spirit of direct observation, to examine their own writing to find the typically personal locations of variable pointers, to assess the effectiveness of those locations, and to weigh the possibility of increased effectiveness of other locations.

5. Second only to metaphor, the construction and location of pointers is among the most significant differences between prose and poetry. (O *wild West Wind,* thou breath *of Autumn's being,*/Thou, *from whose unseen presence* the leaves *dead*/Are driven, *like ghosts from an enchanter fleeing,/Yellow,* and *black,* and *pale,* and *hectic red,/Pestilence-stricken multitudes* . . .)

The results were exactly as Jerome S. Bruner had predicted in *The Process of Education* and *On Knowing* (Harvard, 1961, 1962), those excellent introductions to the inductive method which contain the underlying suppositions for the inductive approach outlined in this article: ". . . to the degree that one is able to approach learning as a task of discovering something rather than 'learning about' it, to that degree there will be a tendency for the child to work with the anatomy of self-reward or, more properly, be rewarded by discovery itself."

Two changes have become apparent in the attitudes of ninety sophomores who participated in the study. They have become intimately familiar with what language is, what it does, and how it does what it does. They have made it work for them in their own papers. And, these students have an overwhelming desire to meet some of the authors of textbooks, particularly those who utter such nonsense as "A preposition is a word used to show the relation of a noun or pronoun to some other word in the sentence."

With the kind permission of Miss Jane Morrisey of New Rochelle, we reproduce below a lesson plan designed to allow students to make the kinds of discoveries Sabol describes:

Purpose of Lesson

To help students formulate a descriptive rule about the order of modification before a noun headword when the headword is modified by a determiner, number word, adjective and noun.

Procedure

A. *When students come into the room, the following clusters will be written on the left-hand side of the board:*

1. tall the three trees oak
2. nine peas those old giant
3. small cakes our birthday four
4. smart six my girl friends

"Here are four groups of words. Do they make any particular sense?"

"Will someone volunteer to make the first cluster make sense?"

(Repeat question and write answers on the right side of the board until the four clusters are in the right order.)

"How did you decide the right order?"

B. *"Now let's examine the clusters and see what has happened."*

"Look at the last word in each cluster: *trees, peas, cakes, friends.*

Are these words alike in any way? Write answer in box above the words.

(Repeat this same procedure until all the words in the cluster have been classified.)

	Det.	number	adj.	noun	noun
1. *tall the three trees oak*	*the*	*three*	*tall*	*oak*	*trees*
2. *nine peas those old giant*	*those*	*nine*	*old*	*giant*	*peas*
3. *small cakes our birthday four*	*our*	*four*	*small*	*birthday*	*cakes*
4. *smart six my girl friends*	*my*	*six*	*smart*	*girl*	*friends*

PROBLEM: To formulate a descriptive rule about the order of modification of nouns.

C. *If you had to say that one of these five words is the most important, which one would you pick?*

"We'll call that word the headword. What kinds of words have we discovered modify the headword?"

"How did we arrive at this conclusion?"

"Which clusters—the ones on the left or the right side of the board?"

"Why didn't we work with the clusters on the left side?"

"How did we put the clusters in order?"

D. *Let's make some conclusions.*

"On the basis of our work with clusters on the left and our ability to make the meaningful clusters in the right rather easily, what can we conclude about word order?"

"Based on what we have observed, can anyone formulate a descriptive rule about the order of modification?" (As answers are received, write them on the board and have students discuss and clarify the rule as needed.)

E. *Assignment.*

"In order to find more evidence supporting what we have said about the modification of nouns, construct ten more clusters like the ones we have been working with; that is, determiner, number word, adjective, noun, noun.

As a final illustration of the sophisticated kind of inquiry that inductive teaching often leads to, let us offer the case of an eleventh-grade teacher who initiated an examination of the role of metaphor in grammar. She began by quoting Sapir's famous caution that "all grammar books leak." To what, she asked the students, was Sapir comparing a grammar? The interesting discussion that ensued led the students to make a list of all the things to which the grammar of a language, as well as language itself, might be compared. To help, the teacher introduced the following poem by Carl Sandburg:

LANGUAGES

There are no handles upon a language
Whereby men take hold of it
And mark it with signs for its remembrance.
It is a river, this language,
Once in a thousand years
Breaking a new course
Changing its way to the ocean.
It is mountain effluvia
Moving to valleys
And from nation to nation
Crossing borders and mixing.
Languages die like rivers.
Words wrapped round your tongue today
And broken to shape of thought
Between your teeth and lips speaking
Now and today
Shall be faded hieroglyphics
Ten thousand years from now.
Sing—and singing—remember
Your song dies and changes
And is not here tomorrow
Any more than the wind
Blowing ten thousand years ago.

She then challenged her students to answer this question: Are Sandburg's metaphors of language useful for the purposes of a grammarian? Eventually, the students examined in some detail the metaphorical assumptions underlying statements of this sort: "A sentence is a complete thought." "A conjunction connects equivalent structures." "An adjective modifies a noun." "A sentence consists of different parts." "There are two kinds of sentences, kernels and transforms."

If these questions seem to verge on the realm of philosophy or metaphysics, bear in mind that they are, nonetheless, relevant questions for grammarians to ask of themselves and their systems. Moreover, the answers to such questions help us to understand why no single grammar will ever be totally adequate to explain a language and, therefore, why we can expect many new grammars in the years ahead.

The major assumption underlying the discovery method in the teaching of grammar is that only through engaging directly in the kind of inquiry process used by grammarians can students understand where grammars come from, why they come, and how they come. It must always be kept in mind that the whole idea of the discovery method is to create for the student a new role in the learning process, a role which demands that he participate seriously in acts of inquiry. Any program that does not place on the student the responsibility for data gathering, inference making, verifying, defining, generalizing, and evaluating defeats the purpose of using the discovery method, and is, by definition, something other than the discovery method, and something other than linguistics.

It remains for us to say that of all the areas of language study, grammar has the least potential for changing the writing and speaking behavior of students. However, when approached in ways we have described, it is extremely valuable in helping students to learn about the processes of observing, classifying, and defining. It is useful in helping students to understand where knowledge comes from, and how and why generalizations change. It is particularly effective in providing students with a perspective on the nature of systems—the purposes of systems, the rules of systems, the underlying assumptions of systems.

CHAPTER 5

Usage

USAGE AND THE LINGUISTS

Molière once wrote about a Frenchman who was amazed to learn that he had been speaking prose all his life. He was delighted, naturally, and began to behave as if French belonged as much to him as to anyone else. From one point of view, the main contribution of linguistics in regard to usage has been to destroy the basis of most beliefs in "a linguistic aristocracy." What is *usage?* As we said before, usage is the study of the attitudes speakers of a language have toward different aspects of their language (e.g., certain pronunciations, words, and grammatical forms). It is also the study of the ways in which people actually use their language. (And, here, usage becomes almost indistinguishable from *dialect geography* and what we have called *linguistic sociology*.)

What are the *attitudes* that people have about language? They are many and various, but an important group of them is expressed by the question "Am I speaking good (or bad) English?" This question has probably been asked thousands of times, usually addressed to persons of authoritative social or educational standing. (An obvious variation of this question is "Am I using good (or bad) grammar?") Simply, the questioner wants to know if he has broken some rule that appears in grammar books. Examples of such rules are:

Don't use "ain't."

Don't use double negatives.

Don't end sentences with prepositions.

Don't begin sentences with "and" or "but."

Don't split infinitives.

Our guess is that although most people who have been to school have heard of such rules, not one in a hundred has any idea of where the rules come from. As we have indicated, most of them were invented by eighteenth-century grammarians and language philosophers, who were guided by several assumptions that can bear repeating: First, change in language represents decay. Second, language is logical, or *should* be logical. Third, the grammar (and "logic") of Latin is the purest of all grammars (and "logics"). Fourth, there are certain forms and sounds of language that are "inherently" better than others. And, finally, the function of grammarians, lexicographers, and other language scholars is to set the rules of "good usage."

Largely through the work of such nineteenth-century and early-twentieth-century linguists as Grimm, Sweet, H. C. Wyld, Jespersen, George Krapp, Bloomfield, and Sapir, strenuous assaults were made on all of these assumptions. Their inquiries into the history of English and other languages led to the belief that change in language is as inevitable as change in everything else. Some linguists, among them Wyld, came to the conclusion that the tendency of language change is in the direction of "infinite variety." Others concluded the opposite—that language changes in the direction of "unity." In any case, it was clear that change is always occurring. Moreover, the causes of change can be identified. For example, Jespersen gives many examples of loan words—cases of one language "borrowing" words from other languages. Grimm and Verner, as we have mentioned, identified regular patterns of phonetic change, and explained these in terms of certain "laws." The principle of "analogic newformations" was shown to be another powerful factor in language change. This term refers to the creation of new forms based on analogy with existing forms. For example, the child who says *foots* instead of *feet* is using the process of analogy, which is exactly what you would do if you attempted to use a form with which you were not familiar. If someone said that he had bought a *kravam,* you would quite naturally assume that if he bought another, he would have two *kravams.* By the same principle, anyone who *kravanates* today will be *kravanating* tomorrow, and probably has *kravanated* in the past. Recently, this process has also operated to change the plural form of *brother* from *brethren* to *brothers.* It seems to be working too to change *oxen* to *oxes.*

The term functional shift has been used to denote a process of change in which one "part of speech" is shifted to function as a different "part of speech." For example, the word *contact* was originally used only as a noun: "The contact was made." Now it is used almost universally as a verb: "I'll contact you tomorrow." *Telephone,* at first a noun, now also functions as a verb: "I telephoned on Tuesday."

Sapir wrote a lucid explanation of still another principle of change, which he called "drift." Drift is the tendency of the structure of a language to continue changing in a particular direction. For example, it is a fact that English has lost many of its inflectional forms (word endings) during the past one thousand years. As English lost its inflections, it relied increasingly on word order to carry the burden of its grammatical information. In particular, the basic structure of the English sentence became Subject-Verb-Object. This tendency caused the change from Chaucer's *It am I* to *It is I,* and is continuing the change to *It is me.* In other words, because the drift of the language is toward S-V-O, forms that are in the "wrong" place (e.g., the predicate nominative, as in "It is *she*"; or *whom* in the subject position, as in, "*Whom* did you see?") are altered to fit the "psychologic" of the language. The word psychologic is intended to suggest that language is governed by rules and and influences that do not correspond to formal logical rules. For example, *everyone* is largely a singular form in America. In England, it is plural. Moreover, in America, although we say "Everyone is here," we also say, "Everyone waved at the President, and he waved back at *them.*" Illogical? Those who impose an arbitrary system of logic on language say Yes. Those who have studied the changing patterns of language say that whatever "logic" there is in language can only be inferred from what has actually happened and is happening to the language.

To take another example, we sometimes hear it said that two negatives make a positive, so that "I don't have none" *really* means "I do have some." Logical? Yes, say those who impose mathematical concepts on language. Nonsense, say those who recognize that in fact "I don't have none" means "I don't have any" to any normal and competent user of the language. Spanish, they point out, uses double negatives even more than English, and Chaucer used triple negatives. The rule that double negatives make a positive may have wide application in algebra; it has very little in natural languages. Another way of saying all of this is that linguists discovered that language is the product of *people;* it is therefore as much governed by psychological and physiological factors as by purely "logical" ones. As Sapir remarked in *Language* (1921), " 'Whom did you see?' might do for an epitaph, but 'Who did you see?' is the natural form for an eager inquiry. It is of course the uncontrolled speech of the folk to which we must look for advance information as to the general linguistic movement."

Thus, historical linguistics challenged many of the basic assumptions of the eighteenth-century grammarians. The next great assault on these assumptions came from *anthropological linguists*—Franz Boas, Bronislaw Malinowski, Bloomfield, Sapir, Whorf, Dorothy Lee. For the most part, their studies were concerned with American Indian languages, such as Algonkian, Navaho, and Hopi. What did they find? They found that there were "laws" governing phonetic change in these languages, just as there were laws governing phonetic change in European languages. Here, to digress for a moment, something should be said about the use of the word *laws* in this context, and no one is better suited to say it than Sapir:

> These phonetic laws are by no means comparable to the laws of physics or chemistry or any other of the natural sciences. They are merely general statements of series of changes characteristic of a given language at a particular time. Thus, a phonetic law applying to a particular sound in the history of English applies only to that sound within a given period of time and by no means commits itself to the development of the same sound at another period in the history of English.

To continue, the anthropological linguists found that the structure of the Indian languages was by no means "primitive."

They found these languages to contain concepts just as "sophisticated" as the concepts of European languages. The Chinookian language, for one, has as much (or as little) complexity as Greek or Latin or English. In short, they concluded that there is no *linguistic basis* for believing that the sound or grammatical system of one language is "logically" or "inherently" superior to any other. Moreover, from the perspective of the study of "primitive" languages, no *linguistic basis* could be found for assuming that any one *dialect* was superior to another. The term linguistic basis is stressed because linguists have always recognized, and continue to recognize, along with everybody else, that certain pronunciations, grammatical forms, and dialects have what might be called a *social superiority;* that is to say, they are valued from a social (or artistic) point of view more than others. Nonetheless, the distinction between a linguistic basis of superiority and a social basis is fundamental. It is one thing to say that *dese, dem,* and *dose* are "wrong" because certain social groups don't use them and don't like to hear them used. It is quite another thing to say that *dese, dem,* and *dose* are inherently less correct than *these, them,* and *those.*

Thus, the cumulative effect of the work of linguists in the matter of usage and correctness has been to call into question most of the beliefs and assumptions that have long been advanced by the schools. It goes without saying, therefore, that the conclusions of linguists were attacked vigorously by many people, particularly those of the social and educational elite. In some of the more extreme cases, a position similar to the following was advanced:

> The truth is, however, that authority of general usage, or even of the usage of great writers, is not absolute in language. There is a misuse of words which can be justified by no authority, however great, and by no usage however general.—R. C. White, *Words and Their Uses.*

This view reminds the authors of a remark made to them by a student: "The truth exists independent of and prior to man, and wouldn't change even if it could." Certainly the statement quoted above is asserting that "correctness" is not a matter that the users of a language can determine; "correctness" exists independent of and prior to man, and wouldn't change even if it could.

Most objections to the conclusions of linguists were not (and are not) as absurd as this. More typically, they take the following line: "The linguists tell us that there is no right or wrong in language, or, even worse, that whatever is in current use is right! Such a point of view is certainly a perverse conception of democracy. It gives license to the perpetration of the worst habits of language usage by the uneducated, and denigrates those who through education and effort use language with care."

Most linguists would answer in some such way as this: "All forms of human behavior are assigned values. The values assigned may differ from culture to culture, but all societies have *preferences* for certain behaviors as against others. Language, a form of human behavior, is no exception. In English, for example, we know that there is a preference for *I don't have any,* as against *I don't have none.* Now, there are four questions to be asked about such a preference. The first is, Who is expressing the preference? The answer, in this case, is: "Certain groups of people, usually those of the middle and upper social classes. The second question is, Why should *their* preference prevail (over that of those whose preference is for *I don't have none*)? Their preference prevails in the matter of language, as in other matters, because they have power—social, economic, and political power. These are the people who have the major responsibilities for running the affairs of the community and *who make decisive judgments about all members of the community.* The third question is, Why do these people prefer certain language forms? The answer to this one is complicated but, in general, we can say custom, or convention, is the determining factor. Why do these people prefer slim ties to wide ones? Why do they prefer to wear tuxedos at weddings and other formal events? The answers are similar to why they prefer *I don't have any* to *I don't have none.*

The fourth question is, Doesn't the research of linguistics yield any basis other than custom or usage for such preferences? The answer is, very little. If one uses communication as a criterion, then it must be admitted that "I don't have none" is not any more ambiguous than "I don't have any." Mathematical logic is largely inapplicable to language so there is no help to be had there. If one uses history as a criterion, the argument might go in favor of "I don't have none," since the double negative has been in use almost eight hundred years. Moreover, the double negative was standard English during Elizabethan times. (So was the double superlative, e.g., "most unkindest.") If one uses economy as a criterion, then "I don't have any" must be given the edge, but bear in mind that all grammars are redundant; that is, they express in different ways the same idea. For example, the sentence "These are my six brothers," has one lexical and three grammatical indications of plurality. Would it be preferable to say, "This is my six brothers"? If style and tone are used as criteria, then we must answer, everything depends on the speaker's purpose and audience. Such concepts as "effective style" and "appropriate tone" are matters of convention, and what is effective and appropriate for one purpose and audience may not be effective and appropriate for another. In other words, it is just as futile to attempt to find inherent value in language forms as it is in, say, the physical form of money. Could you tell which is "better" (i.e., more valuable) a silver coin or a piece of green paper by simply examining the objects themselves? (If anything, you would probably have to say the coin, since it is more durable.) The only way you can sensibly tell which is "better" is by finding out what people *think the objects are worth*. It is the same with language. The "goodness" or "badness" of language is not to be found in the linguistic form itself but in the opinion of those who use the language.

Only someone bent on distortion could conclude from the explanation above that the linguist has done away with concepts of right and wrong in language. He has simply refuted the basis of some of the grounds on which superiority (or inferiority) was claimed to rest. In fact, one of the most important contributions of linguistics in the area of usage is that it has initiated an informed dialogue on the definition of good and bad language.

This process of redefinition has been going on for seventy years and continues to this day. For example, in 1895, Adolph Noreen offered the following definition of good language. (He called his definition the rational or common-sense point of view): "That best is that which can be caught most exactly and most quickly by the audience present and be most easily produced by the speaker." Noreen's emphasis on audience and economy has not been shared by all linguists. Sweet emphasized widespread acceptance: "Whatever is in general use in a language is for that very reason grammatically correct." Jespersen asserted that what is linguistically correct is by definition "that which is demanded by the particular linguistic community to which one belongs. What is at variance with it is linguistically incorrect." Robert Pooley has offered the following: "Good English is that form of speech which is appropriate to the purpose of the speaker, true to the language as it is, and comfortable to speaker and listener. It is the product of custom, neither cramped by rule nor freed from all restraint; it is never fixed but changes with the organic life of the language."

This definition has a historical dimension which our own does not, since it seems to us that the question of "good" English is always a personal one relevant to a particular situation. Nonetheless, our own definition of good English is a variation of Pooley's, and, naturally, like Noreen, we feel it represents the rational and common-sense point of view: "Good English is that which most effectively accomplishes the purposes of the speaker." This view of good English assumes that when a person opens his mouth to speak or raises a pen to write, he has a purpose or purposes in mind. It also assumes that these have something to do with people; that is, we wish to amuse them, or inform them, or confuse them, or insult them, incite them to action, induce inaction or introspection, or a hundred other possible outcomes. It assumes further that people vary in their ages, experience, interests, knowledge, intelligence, social class, and prejudices (linguistic and otherwise). Thus, we conclude, with Jespersen, that "The individual in his use of language has constantly to improvise. He continually finds himself in new situations and has things to express which he has never before met in exactly the same shape." Accordingly, our definition of a user of "good" English is one whose command of a wide range of language styles, dialects, and usages permits him to achieve, through language, the greatest variety of purposes. A corollary of this view is that anyone who uses language that he *knows* will not help him to achieve his purposes is either linguistically limited or irrational.

We trust it is clear to you that neither our definitions nor the definitions of others are official or conclusive. Linguists vary to a great extent in their definitions of such concepts as "good" and "bad" English (and, incidentally, in the implications of their definitions for education). Several important points, however, must be stressed: First, the various definitions derive from a knowledge of what grounds have been discredited or otherwise shown to be impotent. Second, in many cases, what is being redefined is the meaning of "good" or "correct." For example, some linguists mean by "correct" what is more commonly meant by the word "appropriate." Nonetheless, some people refuse to accept the possibility that "correct" can be used as a synonym for, say, "appropriate." They seem to believe that words have single and real meanings. As I. A. Richards would say, there is a peculiar paralysis attending the process of definition. If you define "correct" as "appropriate," they will say, you have only said what is appropriate; what I want to know is what is really correct.

Third, and most important, definitions of "good English" are now open to discussion and further inquiry. This is one of the important contributions of linguistics to the subject.

It remains for us here to discuss still another contribution of linguistics to the field of usage: attempts to ascertain the actual facts about the speech habits of different groups of people. We shall cite here only two, each of which demonstrates a different method of obtaining usage facts, but both of which exemplify the general orientation of the linguistic scientist.

The first was conducted by Charles Carpenter Fries, and published in 1940 under the title *American English Grammar: The Grammatical Structure of Present-Day American English with Especial Reference to Social Differences or Class Dialects.* Fries' objective was to determine what differences, if any, existed among the writings of people of different educational backgrounds. Among his basic problems were these: (1) to categorize groups of people by their educational backgrounds, (2) to obtain natural samples of their writing, (3) to compare and contrast the data, (4) to draw conclusions based on analysis of the data. To give you some idea of the precision with which Fries pursued these objectives, we offer his own description of the procedures used to solve problem one.

> Although we have used for this particular study some two thousand complete letters, and excerpts from about one thousand more, they were all from native Americans for at least three generations. These were arranged in social or class groups in accord with the information available concerning the writers of the letters. Because of the nature of the material used, there is in this study no evidence of what may be termed "literary" language. These were all personal letters written to accomplish an immediate purpose with presumably no thought that they might ever be read by anyone other than the particular person to whom they were directed. On the other hand, there is nothing from the distinctly "illiterate," for, of course, the language of those who cannot read and write must be studied by other means. There remain then three groups or social classes concerning whose language we sought information through these letters. In order to reduce to a minimum the subjective element in classifying our subjects into social or class groups, we have set up some definitely specific criteria and have tried to apply them rigidly. It is perhaps needless to insist that we classified the writers of the letters, not the letters themselves, and *then* studied the language of the specimens from each class.
>
> At the lower level are those we classified in the group for "vulgar" English, the nearly illiterate, hereafter called Group III. For inclusion in this group we depended upon three types of evidence. No one of these three types of evidence was regarded as sufficient to place a subject; he had to qualify under all three to be classified in Group III.
>
> *a*. The record of the schooling. We included in Group III no one who had passed beyond the eighth grade in the schools. Most of our subjects in this group had not attained that level. This statement must not be taken to mean that all who had had only seven or eight years of schooling were

included. This was simply a negative standard; no one who had had more than this amount of schooling was included.

b. The general information concerning the family circumstances. Only those whose occupations were strictly manual and unskilled were included; clerical workers of every sort were ruled out, even those merely clerking in stores. Even strictly manual workers were excluded if their wages amounted to more than ninety dollars a month.

c. Certain definite, formal, non-linguistic matters in the letters themselves. These were matters of spelling, capitalization, and punctuation which clearly demonstrated that the writer was not accustomed to writing at all, that he was semi-illiterate. For this purpose mere accidental misspellings were not considered, but the habitual misspelling of eight or ten simple words was regarded as significant when joined with the evidence from capitalization (lowercase letters for the pronoun *I* and the initial letters of the names of towns and persons), and with the evidence from punctuation (no sentence and punctuation of any kind in a letter of more than two hundred words). Such, for example, was the situation in a letter from 8005. The word *know* was spelled "no" all six times it was used; "rote" for "wrote," three times; "rong" for "wrong," twice; "crect" for "correct"; "prade" for "parade"; "hu" for "who"; "anoff" for "enough"; "parence" for "parents"; "nervice" for "nervous."

Using these three types of evidence together we found specimens from more than three hundred subjects whom we classified in Group III.

At the upper end of the scale were those whom we have classified in the group for "standard" English, the socially acceptable, called hereafter Group I. For inclusion in this group the information available concerning the subject must show that he qualified in all three of the following points:

1. The record of his formal education must show that he is a graduate of one of our reputable colleges after having had at least three years of college life.

2. That his present position must be one of recognized

standing in the community in which he lives. These positions were usually those which are regularly classed as professions and included college professors, physicians, lawyers, judges, clergymen, commissioned officers of the United States Army above the rank of lieutenant, and, from cities of more than 25,000 inhabitants, the superintendents of schools and the editors of newspapers.

3. It is perhaps unnecessary to add that no subjects were put into Group I if the formal, non-linguistic matters in their letters did not conform completely to the usual conventions of written material. As in choosing the subjects for Group III, these non-linguistic matters included spelling, capitalization, and the uses of end punctuation.

No one was accepted as a subject for either Group I or Group III whose record did not meet all the requirements here laid down. The letters of borderline cases were not included in the material to be examined. The purpose of such rigid exclusion from these two groups was to make sure that no serious objections could be raised against the results obtained for either Group I or Group III on the ground that the specimens came from some subjects that might just as well be classified in some other group.

Whether the reader will agree with the names applied to each of these groups does not matter. All will agree, at the very least, that we have here for examination specimens of the language of two very distinct social groups of subjects chosen by the rigid application of certain perfectly definite standards.

Between these two ends of the social scale lies a third class—the great mass of the people in most of our communities—whom we shall call Group II, the users of "common" English. The specimens chosen for examination here come from subjects who may be said to make up the central core of this class which includes the majority of our people. They are those whose record meets the following requirements:

1. They have had a formal education ranging from at least one year of high school to a single year in college or technical school.

2. They are substantial citizens of a community, with occupations that are neither professional on the one hand nor strictly manual and unskilled on the other. They include businessmen, electricians, foremen of large shops, superintendents of mills, heads of police departments, undertakers, Red Cross workers, nurses, and non-commissioned officers of the army of the grade of sergeant. Qualified representatives of other similar occupations would have been included in this group had there been specimens from such subjects in our material. Those listed include all that make up our Group II.

3. In the formal, non-linguistic matters, considered for other groups, the subjects accepted for Group II all conformed with the conventional practice in respect to ordinary capitalization and the end punctuation of sentences. In respect to spelling none were included who like those of Group III habitually misspelled any of the very common words, but occasional misspelling of the common "problem" words or of unusual words did not exclude a subject from this group as it did from Group I.

Note that Fries is describing in this passage his *defining* process. Note, too, that he gives a precise and unevaluative meaning to such terms as "vulgar" and "semi-illiterate." As mentioned in the beginning of the passage, he used as his language sample approximately three thousand letters. (The letters were obtained from the files of the United States government.) Fries categorized his data into three general types of devices to express grammatical ideas. First, the *forms* of words. Second, the uses of *function words*. Third, the uses of *word order*. Examples of the kinds of conclusions his data led him to formulate are as follows:

a. Standard English uses multiple modifiers much more frequently than does Vulgar English. Only eleven instances all told appeared in the Vulgar English materials and these were all either of two or three levelled adjectives or of such words as *last* with a numeral. . . .

b. The Vulgar English of Group III differs sharply from the Standard English of Group I in respect to the form of the word *regard* in the expression *in regard(s) to.* The letters from Group I used only *in regard to.* Those from Group III used *in regards to* much more frequently than *in regard to,* the exact proportion being 69.5 per cent of *regards* to 30.5 per cent of *regard.* Those from Group II also used both *in regard to* and *in regards to* but the form *regard* predominated slightly; the exact proportion was seven of *in regard to* to six of *in regards to.* There may be some connection between this *regards* and the verbal form *regards* in "as regards his ____" which appeared once in the materials of both Group I and Group II but not in those of Group III.

c. Group III differs from Group I in its treatment of the form *lot* meaning "many, a large number." Group I uses only *a lot* as in "thirty letters and *a lot* more" (6514). Group III has *a lots* as in "save *a lots* of lives and money" (8063), or *a lot* without the *of* as in "and *a lot* other things" (8186). Several instances occur without the *a* as "there has been *lots of* sentence cut" (8039) and "you have *lots of* mothers asking for ____" (8187).

I. *This, These, That, Those*

In Group I, the letters of Standard English, *this, these, that, those* as attributives usually agree in form with the form of the noun following. This agreement in form applies even to collective nouns, as "*This throng* of people was gathered to pay *their* tribute to the heroes" (8066). With two words, however, *kind* and *sort* (which may also be considered collectives), the plural forms *these* and *those* very frequently appear in those cases in which a plural noun follows the *of,* as in "*These* kind of letters." The use of *these* and *those* with *kind of* and *sort of* appears here in Group I, the letters of Standard English, but *not once* in Group III, the letters of Vulgar English. The one example in Group III that comes nearest to this use is the sentence "I suppose you get all kind of letters the same as this" (8005).

One other exception to the usual practice of agreement in form of *this, these, that, those* with the nouns they modify shows itself in those situations in which a plural word is taken as a unit, as in "This eleven days was consumed in ____" (9043), and "That twenty-five dollars I had to borrow . . . was . . ." (8288). In this construction the singular form *this* or *that* does not *immediately* precede the plural noun; some other word or words, including a numeral, stand between the singular demonstrative and the plural noun. This practice is not limited to any one of the classes of English examined. It appears equally in all three.

The distinct Vulgar English plural demonstrative form, which, however, appears only four times in the letters is *them* as in "*them* nice little boys" (8187). Paralleling the Standard English use of *these* and *those* it also is used with the words *kind of* and *sort of,* as in "them kind of books."

The second study worth mentioning here was conducted by Sterling A. Leonard, and published in 1932 under the title *Current English Usage*. Leonard's objective was to ascertain the actual usage of cultivated people, *according to the judgment of certain groups.* He solicited the opinions of seven groups of people on whether or not certain constructions were "acceptable," "disputable," or "illiterate." He did not ask them to comment on whether or not such constructions *should* be acceptable, but on whether they, in fact, *were,* based on their own observaton of the language behavior of educated people. His seven groups were: language scholars, active members of the National Council of Teachers of English, well-known authors, editors, businessmen, members of the Modern Language Association, and teachers of speech. Essentially, Leonard used the questionnaire as his instrument of inquiry; his data were the opinions of people whom he had defined as "educated" or "cultivated."

Neither Fries nor Leonard urged that people use language any way they care to. In fact, the basic assumption underlying their work is that people place different values on different kinds of language. The result of their work was to provide a more precise understanding of the differences among varying dialects and styles of language.

In summary, then, the main contributions of linguists engaged in the study of "correctness" and usage are these:

1. They have called into serious question the major assumptions of eighteenth-century grammarians on matters of language change, the bases of correctness, and the status of logic and Latin.

2. They have initiated an informed dialogue on the question "What are legitimate criteria on which to base a conception of good and bad usage?"

3. They have provided reliable information about the characteristics of different dialects and styles of language.

USAGE AND WRITING IN THE SCHOOLS

In 1925, Leonard Bloomfield wrote, "Our schools are conducted by persons who, from professors of education to teachers of classrooms, know nothing of the results of linguistic science." Twenty years later, Charles Fries observed that the situation had not changed much. He said, "The views of language that prevail in the schools and among even the 'educated' public still perpetuate the authoritarian attitude of the eighteenth century." What is the situation today? In brief, we find three kinds of approaches to the study of usage. First, there exists, to a depressing extent, teachers who have been totally unaffected by anything that has happened in language scholarship. They regard such terms as "correct" and "incorrect" English as absolutes, perhaps even believing that correct English "exists prior to and independent of man." They provide students with lists of expressions that are labeled "incorrect," which the students are commanded to avoid using. They view changes in language as corruptions. They stand firmly on Latin and logic as the basis for correctness. They attach moral connotations to "good" and "bad" English. The kind of student they often produce is described extremely well by S. I. Hayakawa in the following passages from his article "Linguistic Science and the Teaching of Composition":

> The most common result of the teaching of English and composition is not the creation of good writers and speakers, but the creation, in most of the public, of a lifelong fear of grammatical errors. . . . To be sure, we help some

of our students to speak and write better. But the majority of fair-to-middling students leave the English class feeling that "correct English," like moral perfection, is something that they cannot hope to attain. Burdened, as the result of our castigations, by a sense of linguistic Original Sin, they depart from school feeling, like those Puritans who felt that whatever was fun must be sinful, that whatever sounds natural must be wrong. It is tragic that most Americans suffer, with respect to the use of their own language, especially in formal or semi-formal situations, a discomfort or malaise that can only be described as a mild form of anxiety neurosis. . . . I vividly remember a student of mine, an elementary school teacher, who, when asked to write a theme in class, went into a more than usually acute anxiety state. In the course of 50 minutes, she wore four or five holes in the first two lines of her sheet of paper with repeated erasures; she chewed an eight-inch pencil down to two inches; she displayed the classic psychosomatic symptoms of anxiety, trembling, flushing, and sweating. At the end of the period there was nothing on her paper but the marks of erasure and a large moist blur of sweat where her hand had been. Every teacher of English is able to recall similar instances. We have all experienced, too, the embarrassed silence that occurs among many social groups when they find that an English teacher is in their midst, and I am sure we have all felt the need to publicly split an infinitive or two in order to dispel that anxiety. I mention these familiar experiences in order to underline the fact that, in linguistic as in other behavior, when people do not know how to act and cannot figure out how to discover how to act, and when previous attempts to act appropriately have repeatedly been met with failure or censure, the result cannot but be some kind of anxiety state. Just as the old-fashioned, two-valued morality of absolute evil was charged by Dr. Oliver Wendell Holmes to be a contributory cause of mental illness—an observation deeply confirmed by psychiatric science many decades later—so does it now appear that the old-fashioned, two-valued grammar of "correct" versus "incorrect"

> English is a contributory cause of the more or less grave linguistic neuroses that most people suffer from.

Even if one is not willing to accept Hayakawa's linking of neurotic behavior with the teaching of a "two-valued" conception of usage, it is almost a certainty that this approach to usage fails to produce students who are curious about language, who have knowledge about how it works, and who can use it with resourcefulness. However, it is probably true that time is running against such an approach as this. Although it is astonishing how resourceful some people are in maintaining their ignorance, the increasing interest in linguistics is bound to affect all teaching of English in the years ahead.

The second kind of teacher is one who has been affected by linguistics, but not by its emphasis on inquiry. These teachers frequently think of themselves as "liberals" in matters of usage. They have reduced the list of proscribed forms because they recognize that "educated people" no longer disapprove of some of the expressions that students traditionally have been commanded not to use. For example, the conservative teacher tells her students that "Will everyone please put on their coats?" is wrong. The liberal teacher tells her students that it is right. The latter can be more harmful in some ways than the teacher who knows nothing of linguistics. Whereas the traditionalist makes no pretense of doing or saying anything new, the liberal does. Thus, under the banner of a "new English" or the "linguistic approach," classes are conducted in the same old way.

From the standpoint of our definition of linguistics, neither of these two types of teachers understands linguistics very well. Both are stifling the very essence of linguistics, which is inquiry. Moreover, both teachers are dogmatists, although (if you will forgive the pun) their dogmas differ in detail. The result of what they are doing is to leave the student with no desire, no opportunity, and no methodology with which to challenge or question what he is told. Learning about usage is for him an act of obedience, not of inquiry. It is true that the "liberal" teacher's student is provided with more accurate information about the facts of his language, but, in our view, he pays too high a price.

The third kind of teacher is the one whose activities are worth publicizing. He is the teacher who accepts the following assumptions (some of them borrowed from G. Robert Carlsen's article "Conflicting Assumptions in the Teaching of English"):

1. While there is a core of commonality in the language of a group, the language is subject to almost infinite variations among its users.

2. There are no permanent, absolute rules for English, since it is constantly changing.

3. Language is primarily a form of behavior, learned best by observation and use.

4. One learns about the "goodness" or "badness" of language by observing its effects on people.

5. The function of the teacher is to help students make effective language decisions by helping them to become good observers of how language works.

The accounts and descriptions which follow, then, are of classrooms whose teachers are using what may rightly be called a "linguistic approach" to usage.

In a ninth-grade class in New York City, a teacher led his students to conduct a serious inquiry into the question "Who or what determines correctness in language?" The first task of the students was to define what "correctness" or "rightness" means in the context of language. Is linguistic correctness a social problem? a political problem? a theological problem? a moral problem? a physiological problem? The students tried to answer these questions by contrasting the meanings of the word "correct" as it appeared in different contexts (e.g., a "correct" solution to a mathematical problem; a "correct" judicial decision; a "correct" political policy). Quite obviously, the first thing the students were learning was that the meanings of words are not fixed and that the context in which they appear is decisive.

It is worth remarking here that a good deal of the theological or moral overtones of most discussions of usage are probably accounted for by the connotation of the words *good* and *bad,* as in "good grammar" and "bad grammar." Teachers have rarely helped students make a distinction between the meanings of *good* in "good grammar" and "a good girl" or of *bad* in "bad grammar" and "a bad girl." In the class we are describing, the teacher spent several class sessions working on the problem of definitions. As a consequence, the students came to understand that one of the basic steps in the inquiry process is a careful definition of key terms. In this particular class, several definitions of correct English were arrived at, each definition leading to a different inquiry. For example, some students defined correct English as "the speech and writing of educated people." Once having done that, they immediately perceived that their next question had to be "How does one determine who is an educated person?" which was followed by the question "How does one find out what the language of educated people is?" Their attempts to answer this last question led them out into their community, to handbooks of usage, to dictionaries, to their television sets, to newspapers, to plays and films, from all of which they gathered linguistic data on which to base generalizations about the language of educated people.

Another group of students defined correct English as "the English we are told to use by grammar books and dictionaries." This definition led them to ask such questions as "Who writes grammar books and dictionaries?" "Do all grammar books and dictionaries agree?" "What changes, if any, have taken place in grammar books and dictionaries on the matter of what is or is not correct English?"

Other definitions of correct English were also given and each in its turn generated further questions that, of course, became the basis for serious inquiry. Two aspects of the work of this class must be stressed. The first is that, as they proceeded with their work, the students were answering many questions other than the specific ones they were trying to solve. For example, it has already been mentioned that the youngsters had to deal with problems of definition. They also had to deal with certain problems of social attitudes and individual prejudice. Teachers who have allowed students to participate in inquiries into usage soon discover that the students have internalized certain attitudes that often block them from an objective examination of matters of usage. For example, one student insisted that you could define correct English all day and in a hundred different ways but it still really meant what the dictionary or grammar book said it was. Apparently this student had so deeply internalized this particular meaning of correctness in language that he was unable to shift his point of view even for the purpose of an objective inquiry.

The second aspect of this class that needs to be especially commented on concerns the role of the teacher. He perceived his function as that of one who is there to help students conduct their inquiries. In other words, his job was to give structure to the students' attempts to ask questions, to observe, define, verify, and generalize. He was not interested in imposing a point of view on the students, except in so far as it was a point of view that insists upon honest and rigorous investigation of a problem.

Another teacher, in Anaheim, California, helped his tenth-grade students to conduct an inquiry into the differences in usage that existed in their community. Below is an example of the questionnaire that was devised and administered by students and whose results were evaluated by students.

Questionnaire

I. Please indicate how you feel about the italicized word or expression in each of the following sentences by placing a check in the appropriate box.

	RIGHT	WRONG	UNCERTAIN
1. It is *me.*	☐	☐	☐
2. Everyone please put on *their coats.*	☐	☐	☐
3. He *don't* influence me.	☐	☐	☐
4. *Who* did you see yesterday?	☐	☐	☐
5. He will come before you *will have finished* your work.	☐	☐	☐
6. I *am going to go* tomorrow.	☐	☐	☐
7. I *shall* go tomorrow.	☐	☐	☐
8. Neither you nor he *is* tall.	☐	☐	☐
9. Let's keep this between *you* and I.	☐	☐	☐
10. This is the *most unkindest* thing you have ever done.	☐	☐	☐
11. Winstons taste good *like* a cigarette should.	☐	☐	☐
12. That's a *real* good curve ball.	☐	☐	☐

	RIGHT	WRONG	UNCERTAIN
13. It is *not unlikely* that he will come.	☐	☐	☐
14. Each of the boys *are* coming to the party.	☐	☐	☐
15. I *will* go tomorrow.	☐	☐	☐
16. He *doesn't* have *no* money.	☐	☐	☐
17. To *myself,* this seems silly.	☐	☐	☐

II. We would also appreciate your giving us the following information:

1. Where were you born?
2. Name the schools you have attended.
3. Was or is English one of your favorite school subjects?
4. What is your occupation?

Although the questionnaire as a method of inquiry has its limitations, it is worth remembering that one of the earliest studies of usage, Sterling A. Leonard's, used the questionnaire as a means of accumulating data.

Another teacher in Minneapolis had his eleventh-grade students make inquiries into each of the following standards of usage. (The teacher obtained the list from Jespersen's *Mankind, Nation and Individual.*)

1. the standard of authority
2. the geographical standard
3. the literary standard
4. the aristocratic standard
5. the democratic standard
6. the logical standard
7. the aesthetic standard

The students tried to discover what is meant by each of these standards. Why have people deferred to them? What effect has any particular standard had on the language? Are any of these reasonable and useful standards of "correctness"?

The students' inquiries not only led them to read Jespersen's discussions of these standards, but led them to read the prefaces of dictionaries and the usage sections of several grammar books. Some of the more able students pursued the matter from a historical perspective, referring to eighteenth- and nineteenth-century dictionaries, as well as twentieth-century works.

A ninth-grade teacher in Long Island had her students replicate, with appropriate variations, the study conducted by Fries. The students used as their data letters published in the Letters to the Editor columns of three newspapers, *The New York Times,* the *New York Post,* and the *New York Daily News.* Somewhat arbitrarily, they equated the writers to the *Times* with Fries' Group I, the writers to the *Post* with Group II, and writers to the *News* with Group III. They classified their data into three categories: differences in word forms, word order, and function words. In addition to writing a report on their findings, the students were required to write an account of the entire inquiry. Their report included a careful statement of the problem, a description of the assumptions underlying the investigation, their definitions of key terms, and a description of the procedures used, with special emphasis on the kinds of observations they made.

What are the students in these classes learning? First of all, they learn what even the most traditional teacher wants them to learn, namely, that there are value judgments made about different ways of using language. Moreover, the students quickly learn what language forms are judged unacceptable. But, unlike students in a traditional class, these students also learn where the judgments come from. In addition, they learn that judgments about usage are often controversial and, in any case, will differ depending on who is making the judgment. It goes without saying that sociological implications of assertions about usage do not go unnoticed by students. For example, it was quite easy for the students who administered the questionnaire or those who replicated Fries' study to see that attitudes toward language forms are correlated with social class.

In fact, several students in these classes were led to the conclusion that "our attitudes toward language forms are in direct proportion to our attitudes toward the *people* who use these languages forms." In one class this became known as Feinstein's Law, since a student by that name was the first member of the class to enunciate the generalization. Jespersen, Fries, or Pooley probably could not have said it better.

In another class, a principle that became known as Gorlick's Law was expressed by a student of that name. So far as the authors are aware, Gorlick's Law has never been enunciated by any professional linguist. It is as follows: "Our attitudes toward language are determined to a large extent by the metaphors we use to describe different varieties of language." Gorlick contended, for example, that the phrase "levels of usage" is no improvement on the categories "correct" and "incorrect," since levels implies "higher" and "lower," thus still possessing moralistic connotations. With the kind permission of Alan Criswell, Gorlick's teacher, we have reproduced below the first lesson plan of the series that resulted in, among other things, the formulation of Gorlick's Law.

Asking Questions About Language

The main purpose of this lesson will be to have students learn something of the art of asking questions about language. On the board as the period opens will be the following two statements: (1) Change in language leads to corruption of a language. (2) Change in language leads to improvement of a language.

We shall begin the lesson with a brief introduction along the following lines: You may recall when we talked about the great lexicographer of the English language, Samuel Johnson, that we found that he believed that language change resulted in corruption of our language. But was Johnson correct? Perhaps language change leads to improvement of our language. In any case, you see on the board two contradictory statements. Perhaps neither one of them is true, but it does not seem likely that both can be true. What questions can we raise about these two statements which, if answered factually, would lead us to the truth?

As students raise questions about the two statements, their questions will be written on the board. Next, we shall consider the questions themselves: How good are they? How relevant? Do any of them contain assumptions which we have not established as true? Finally, we shall try to determine which of the questions furnishes the logical starting point for our inquiry.

This question will probably be one relating to the kinds of change which occur in language. We shall list on the board such kinds of changes which a language may undergo and conclude the lesson with a brief summary statement.

Note that Mr. Criswell did not apparently plan to have students inquire into the role of metaphor in the study of usage. The discussion of this subject developed quite naturally from what the students were doing. Note, too, that Criswell was interested in having his students learn something about the skill and art of asking questions, as well as learning about processes of change in language. (It is worth remarking here that most students go through sixteen years of "education," from kindergarten through college, without ever being given any systematic instruction in how to ask questions!) Finally, note that Criswell invited his students to question authority (Johnson's) and to seek satisfactory answers for themselves.

The inductively oriented teacher of writing quite naturally makes the study of composition and speech a series of problems for students to solve. Such a teacher does not tell his students what is or is not effective speaking or writing. Instead, he persistently raises the questions "If you say or write this, what will be the consequences of your decision?" "Will your purposes for speaking or writing be served by the choice you have made?" "What factors must you take into account before making a language choice?" Naturally, finding the answers to these questions absorbs a great deal of the students' time and energy and, more important, teaches the students to rely on themselves as observers, analysts, and evaluators of the ways in which language affects people, including themselves.

Linguistics and writing. In discussing the applications of linguistics to the teaching of writing, we must stress at the outset two points. First, it is sometimes said that the linguistic approach to writing (and to usage) implies that "anything goes." In point of fact, this approach implies just the opposite. It implies that in our attempts to communicate with one another almost everything is significant, and that the study of writing (and speaking) is an inquiry into those factors that help or hinder us in achieving our purposes.

The traditional teacher, who is most likely to say that either linguistics or inductive teaching leads to anarchy in language, usually poses for his students such a problem as the following:

Choose the correct form in the following sentences:

1. (Who, Whom) did you see?
2. Everyone please put on (his, their) (coat, coats).
3. I want you to do this (like, as) I do it.

We would submit that this kind of problem represents a simple-minded approach to usage and writing, since it excludes a consideration of all the human factors involved in rendering a language choice either "correct" or "incorrect." These factors include: who you think you are; what you would like others to think you are; what kinds of people you are addressing; your attitude toward them; your judgment of what they expect; and, of course, your purposes. Any teaching of writing which leaves out such considerations is unrealistic, and therefore misleading.

Wendell Johnson was fond of pointing out that "you can't write writing," by which he meant that one is always writing *about* something, a fact which has yet to be discovered by many teachers. But to this fact one needs to add that *you* are always writing to or for *someone,* for a presumably human *purpose.* Thus, the act of writing is not simply a matter of being "clear" or "well organized" or "interesting." Clear to whom? Well organized for whom? Interesting to whom, and for what purposes? The study of writing is the study of human behavior, with particular emphasis on the ways in which language affects that behavior. And what could be more complicated than that?

In a recently published series of "linguistics" texts intended for the third through sixth grades, the author points out that "anything less than a frontal attack—a patient and deliberate explanation of the system—has the effect of putting most of the burden of learning to write English on the child." He goes on to say that his texts will help to reduce, or even remove, that burden. From our point of view, to the extent that "the burden of learning to write English" is *not* on the child, to that extent will he fail to learn how to write. No one and nothing can assume the learner's burden in learning how to write, speak, think, or do anything else. The approach we have been describing is designed to help the learner accept that burden, to deal with it efficiently, and, hopefully, to transform his burden into an opportunity.

The examples we cite below are taken from classrooms in which the burden of learning how to write English rests on the students. The role of the teachers is to keep the burden just where it is.

A junior-high-school teacher in Minnesota, recognizing the critical role of context in effective writing, drew her students' attention to the various factors operating in any language situation by posing the following problems. (She began with problems in speaking rather than writing simply because speech is a more vital part of the students' daily experience than writing.)

In the problems which follow, you will be asked to determine the purposes and consequences of language choices which people make every day. Study each of the following situations and the choices that are given for each. Decide which of the choices you would make and why.

Problem 1

The situation:

You have arrived at the home of a girl you are going to take out on a date. Although you admire the girl very much, you do not think you will like her father. The girl has told you that her father dislikes people who work with their hands for a living. Your father owns a gas station in town. While you are waiting for your date, you meet her father in the living room. After some polite exchange of greetings, her father asks you what *your* father does for a living.

Your language choices:

1. "He's a grease monkey."
2. "He's an auto mechanic."
3. "He's in business for himself."
4. "He's an automotive engineer."

Problem 2

The situation:

You are attending a basketball game with a boy you like very much. One of the players, Ed Shannon, dribbles equally well with both his right and left hands. Your boyfriend turns to you and says, "I've never seen a player as amphibious as Shannon."

Your language choices:

1. "Amphibious? You *must* be kidding! That means something that can live on land and in water."
2. "I think you mean ambidextrous, Bob."
3. "Yes, he is amphibious, isn't he?"
4. "Yes, he is *ambidextrous,* isn't he?"

Problem 3

The situation:

You and two of your close friends are confronted by a man on the street who is soliciting contributions for a worthy cause. None of you has any money. One of your friends says to the man, "I ain't got no money." The man says to your second friend, "Won't you contribute a little?" He replies, "I ain't got no money either." Finally the man turns to you for a contribution.

Your language choices:

1. "I'm like the others. I ain't got no money."
2. "I'm afraid I do not have any money."
3. "Sorry, I'm busted too."
4. "I'd like to contribute, but I'm financially embarrassed at the moment."

Problem 4

The situation:

You are being interviewed for a part-time job. The job is important to you because you know you will need the money in the weeks to come. At one point in the interview, your prospective employer says to you, "I hope working on Saturdays don't bother you."

Your language choices:

1. "No, it don't matter to me."

2. "Working on Saturdays *doesn't* bother me."
3. "No, it doesn't."
4. "No, it don't."

What is happening here? In the first place, students are given confirmation of their intuition that "goodness" or "badness" in language is a function of one's purpose and audience. As a teacher from Portland, Oregon, expressed it: "Actually, most students are aware that they are constantly faced with the necessity of making a choice, often among several usages, but calling attention to this facet of language never fails to achieve an effect. From there it is an easy step to the exploration of the way in which a user of the language makes his choices." In other words, what is happening is that students are engaged in exploring the ways in which language choices are made. In the second place, such an exploration requires, above all, observation of the responses called forth by various language forms and styles. Third, such an exploration requires, too, an increased awareness of one's own purposes in using language. Typical responses to some of the problems given above are these:

"Why should I set myself apart from my friends?"

"Listen, if that guy is a snob, why should I give in to him?"

"Well, if I needed the job bad enough, I'd probably use 'He don't.' "

"It would be rude for me to insult the boy, especially if I really liked him."

Such responses as these represent the beginnings of intelligent analyses of language situations. The transition from such analyses of speech to similar analyses of writing is easily accomplished.

The same Minnesota teacher posed the following reading and writing problems for her students, shortly after they had explored the "language decision" problems:

Problem 1

When you write a letter, you must always be sure that it is in good taste. White stationery, for example, is always in good taste. Never use purple, red, or green ink. Never write letters in pencil and never use ruled paper as letter stationery. Friendly letters should be written in longhand. You should, however, typewrite friendly letters if your handwriting is difficult to read. When you are writing a letter, avoid cross-outs, ink blots, uphill writing, and crowded lines.

Answer the following questions:

1. What are the purposes of the passage above?
2. What words help you to know what the author's purposes are?
3. Do the words *always* and *never* help to clarify the author's purposes? How?
4. Does the author have a specific audience in mind? What relationship does he have to his audience?
5. Can you find an example of language in your classroom that attempts to serve the same purposes as the passage above?
6. In what situations are you likely to use language in this way for these purposes?
7. How well does this passage achieve its purposes?

Problem 2

The following directive was prepared by an assistant in the personnel office of a large corporation where lateness was becoming a major problem. Read it carefully.

"Beginning next Monday, all employees must arrive precisely on time for work. Precisely means 9:00 A.M. It does not mean 9:01 A.M The stockholders of this company expect their employees to work a full seven hours each day, with *one* hour allotted for lunch. Each employee is paid his weekly salary on the assumption that he is working 35 hours per week. Beginning Monday, each employee will have deducted from his pay check whatever portion of his salary his lateness warrants. If, through lateness, he misses one hour of work for that week, one hour's worth of his salary will be deducted from his check."

When the Personnel Manager read this directive, he felt its harsh tone would have a demoralizing effect on the employees and perhaps lead to antagonism instead of cooperation. The problem you must solve is as follows: Rewrite the directive so that its message will be clear and its tone will elicit maximum cooperation from the employees.

After several weeks, the students were engaged in working out relatively sophisticated writing assignments. One of these follows:

Below are four composing situations. Each of them provides you with a subject to write on, a point of view to write from, and an audience to write for. Choose *two* of these problems, decide upon your purpose for writing, and use the form of communication which best suits your purpose. For example, you may wish to write a personal letter, a business letter, a diary entry, a short essay, an advertisement, a telephone conversation, or a face-to-face dialogue.

1. Write a description of your school, from your own point of view, to a person of your age who lives in a foreign country and knows nothing about American schools.
2. Write a description of your school, from your own point of view, to the principal of your school.
3. Write a description of your school, from the point of view of the principal of your school, to the parents whose children attend the school.
4. Write a description of your school, from the point of view of a teacher in the school, to a friend of hers who teaches in another part of the country.

Answer the following questions for each pair of writing assignments you have done:

1. How did your purposes change as you shifted from one point of view to another?
2. What factors determined your purpose in each case?
3. In what ways did your tone change?
4. What factors determined your choice of tone in each case?
5. In what ways did you change your vocabulary and usage?

6. What factors determined your choice of vocabulary and usage in each case?
7. In what ways did your sentence structure change?
8. What factors determined your choice of sentence structure?
9. Is there a description of a school that is more accurate than any other description? In other words, are both of your descriptions in each problem equally accurate?
10. What were the limitations of each of your descriptions?
11. How did the limitations of the audience restrict what the describer could say?
12. How did the prejudices of the describer restrict him?

A ninth-grade teacher in Westchester County (N.Y.) led his students to explore the relationship between the writer's purpose and tone and his use of sentence structure by giving them a series of reading and writing problems to solve. Three of them, focusing on the effects of the passive voice, appear below:

Problem 1

Following is the opening paragraph of a short story, "The Great Wall of China," by Franz Kafka. Read it carefully.

The Great Wall of China was finished off at its northernmost corner. From the south-east and the south-west it came up in two sections that finally converged there. This principle of piecemeal construction was also applied on a smaller scale by both of the two great armies of labor, the eastern and the western. It was done in this way: gangs of some twenty workers were formed who had to accomplish a length, say, of five hundred yards of wall, while a similar gang built another stretch of the same length to meet the first. But after the junction had been made the construction of the wall was not carried on from the point, let us say, where this thousand yards ended; instead the two groups of workers were transferred to begin building again in quite different neighborhoods. Naturally in this way many great gaps were left, which were only filled in gradually and bit by bit, some, indeed, not till after the official announcement that the wall was finished. In fact it is said that there are gaps which have never been filled in at all, an assertion, however, which is probably merely one more of the many legends to which the building of the wall gave rise, and which cannot be verified, at least by any single man with his own eyes and judgment, on account of the extent of the structure.

Answer the following questions:

1. Who "finished off" the Great Wall of China? How far must you read until you can answer?
2. Who directed the formation of the gangs of workers? Do you know?
3. Who was in command of the building of the wall? Do you know?
4. Who transferred the groups of workers to different locations? Do you know?
5. Does the narrator think the wall itself, the people building it, or the people directing its construction are more important? How do you know?
6. Can you relate your answers to Questions 1 to 5 to the sentence structure of the paragraph?

Problem 2

In your notebook, list all the verbs in the paragraph you have just read. Then, rewrite the paragraph, changing the structure of the sentences so that all the verbs are in the active voice. Your paragraph might begin:

> The two great armies of labor finished off the Great Wall of China at its northernmost corner.

Problem 3

Compare your version of the paragraph with the original by answering the following questions:

1. How do the purposes of the two versions differ?
2. How does the tone of your version differ from that of the original?
3. Is there a difference in emphasis between your version and the original? Explain.

In Pittsburgh, another junior-high-school teacher gave his students the following problems at the end of a year's work with problems similar to those described in the preceding pages:

Problem 1

Following is a speech that the Governor's former and now unemployed speech writer prepared for him. You are to make suggestions as to how it can be improved. The speech is to be delivered to the State Association of Teachers and Educators.

Ladies and Gentlemen:

I don't need to tell you how pleased I am to have been invited here to address you at this, your annual convention. You folks are, as the saying goes, the cream of the pack and it is always a special challenge to talk to you, particularly during a real rough political campaign.

I guess you know what it is I want to talk to you about. My subject is teachers' salaries. Now I want you to know—I guess some of you know this already—that I used to be a school teacher myself. I know that it isn't easy living on a teacher's salary. In other words, my friends, I am sympathetic to your cause. I am a friend of the teachers and educators in this state. My record speaks for itself. It really does. When I was in the state legislature, I used to say to my colleagues, "Show me a poorly paid teacher and I'll show you an unhappy teacher."

Now, ladies and gentlemen, I am not the kind of person who makes wild promises. It would be easy for me to say to you on this occasion that if I am re-elected, you'll all get real good salary increases. But, after all, we only have a certain amount of money in the state cash register and everyone, so to speak, seems to have their hands in the old till. But I think I can promise you that if I am re-elected—heck, *when* I am re-elected—you'll all get a pretty good shake. Nothing sensational, mind you. Maybe not even anything terrific. But you'll all get something, and even if you only get an increase of a dollar a week, that would be more than my opponent can give you.

And so, ladies and gentlemen, as my uncle Jonas used to say, "I can't promise you pie in the sky, but I can promise you meat in the pot." That's why I want your vote on Election Day, so that Election Day becomes *Re*-election Day. Thank you.

Problem 2

Choose one of the four pairs of topics below, and write a speech suitable for each subject and audience in the pair you have chosen:

	SUBJECT	AUDIENCE
1.	The importance of the United Nations	The Committee for America's Withdrawal from the United Nations
	Withdrawal from the United Nations	The Committee for Strengthening the United Nations
2.	Increasing government spending	National Association of Independent Businessmen
	Decreasing government spending	Association of Civil Service Employees
3.	Elimination of all obstacles to vigorous law enforcement	Association of Criminal Defense Lawyers
	Increasing safeguards for those accused of crimes	Association of State District Attorneys
4.	Government subsidized medical care	State Association of Physicians and Surgeons
	Keeping government out of the medical profession	The Council for State Social Workers

What all of these teachers are aiming at, of course, is to help develop their students' ability as observers, evaluators, speakers, and writers of language. They recognize that dependence on authority ultimately fails because students must live most of their lives without an English teacher or handbook of usage and composition near by. They recognize that their students must come to do without them.

CHAPTER 6

Semantics

> Since the concepts people live by are derived only from perceptions and from language and since the perceptions are received and interpreted only in the light of earlier concepts, man comes pretty close to living in a house that language built, located by maps that language drew, and linguistics is—or should be—one of the sciences most useful in extending the limits of human knowledge (inquiry, research) and in extending knowledge to humans (education). In thinking about the basic dilemmas of our culture, there would seem to be no more important science than linguistics.
>
> —RUSSELL F. W. SMITH,
> *Linguistics in Theory—and in Practice*

SEMANTICS AND THE LINGUISTS

Perhaps the most important branch of linguistics, as the quotation above suggests, is semantics. In general, semantics is concerned with problems of meaning, the maps that language draws. This concern can be traced back at least to the Greeks in Western civilization, and it is from the Greek word *semantikos* that the term *semantics* derives. *Semantikos* means "significant meaning." The infinitive, *semainein,* from *sema,* "a sign," means "to mean, or to signify." Semantics probably originated at the time when man became aware that he was using language as his primary mode of codifying and communicating meaning. This awareness was undoubtedly provoked by "problems in communication," most of which are still with us. And this is not surprising, since it is difficult to imagine anything more curious—and complex—than the ways in which a "connection" is made between a sound in the air and "meaning." It is essentially this connection that provides the focus for semantic study. In modern times, there have been three major categories of semantics, although there have been many more than three names for them.

First, and oldest of the formal studies, is philology, the study of changes in meanings historically. This was originally called semasiology. The most obvious finding of philological inquiries is that while words may stay the same in form, the meanings given to them can and do change drastically.

Second, and now most closely related to symbolic logic, is what might be called the philosophical approach to the study of meaning. The focus here is on describing and stating "laws" under which language may be regarded as meaningful.

Third, and currently the category in which most activity is occurring, might be called the "scientific" approach to the study of meaning. This form of semantics is largely concerned with the relationships among language, thought, and behavior. Its basic assumption is that the language user is the source of whatever meanings language has.

A brief chronology of semantics in modern times might help to provide a clearer view of the complexities characterizing these branches of linguistics.

While the term *semantics* was not specifically used by him, Alexander Bryan Johnson (1786–1867), of Utica, New York, addressed himself to problems of meaning in the early part of the nineteenth century. In 1836, he published *A Treatise on Language, or the Relation Which Words Bear to Things,* a version of lectures he had been giving for more than ten years. In 1854, *The Meaning of Words: Analyzed into Words and Unverbal Things,* also by Johnson, was published. He was virtually ignored by his contemporaries, but he has recently been rediscovered by doctoral-degree candidates, and as a consequence some of his writings are back in print. Johnson can now be regarded as a forerunner of pragmatism, America's primary contribution, so far, to Western philosophy.

Following Johnson, at least chronologically (since there is no evidence that he was aware of him or his work), Charles Saunders Peirce (1839–1914) also addressed himself to semantic problems. Like Johnson, Peirce did not use the term *semantics*. And, also like Johnson, Peirce's work was largely ignored by his contemporaries, with one notable exception—William James.

Peirce's study of meaning revolves about and extends from his central point that the meaning of abstractions is found only in *use*. The meaning of a term, he believed, is to be found by observing what a man does with it, not by what he says about it. In other words, an abstraction (sign, symbol, idea, etc.) "means" whatever effect it produces when *used*, or when put into operation. Peirce's purpose was to develop a method for the determination of the meaning of terms and propositions in order to distinguish meaningful from nonmeaningful hypotheses. The method he developed for this purpose, Peirce called *pragmaticism*. He felt this term was "ugly enough to be safe from kidnappers." He was wrong. Nonetheless, Peirce's mode of defining—the operational mode—has been regarded by some scientists (for example, P. W. Bridgman) as an intellectual step forward of about the same magnitude as the idea of zero.

The specific word *semantics* appears to have occurred first in *Essai de Sémantique*, a work by the French linguist Michel Bréal (1832–1915), published in 1897. This was translated into English, and thereafter the term *semantics* appeared frequently in publications dealing with problems of meaning. (Bréal, incidentally, confined the term to "laws governing changes of meanings.")

In 1903, Lady Viola Welby published *What is Meaning?* in England. She used the term *significs*, by which she meant "the science of meaning or the study of significance, provided sufficient recognition is given to its practical aspect as a method of mind." It is worth noting, in the light of present developments, that Lady Welby was motivated largely by her interest in improving education. She objected strongly to what she called the "senseless formalism" of teaching procedures which emphasized, almost exclusively, verbalization.

Also in England, in 1910, Alfred North Whitehead and Bertrand Russell produced *Principia Mathematica.* Whitehead and Russell, however, were primarily concerned with resolving some logical contradictions that seemed to resist solution because of inadequacies in the modes of stating certain propositions; that is, the source of the contradictions was viewed as being the language in which the propositions were stated. Here, Whitehead and Russell were coming to grips with the fact that many well-known paradoxes of logic arise when a system tries to deal with itself.

Again in England, C. K. Ogden and I. A. Richards published *The Meaning of Meaning* (1923), in which they probed "the central problem of meaning, the relations of thought and language." Ogden and Richards were motivated, in part, by the timidity of contemporary linguists in dealing with significant language problems. As they note in their Preface:

> Amongst grammarians in particular a sense of uneasiness has prevailed. It has been felt that the study of language as hitherto conducted by traditional methods has failed to face fundamental issues in spite of its central position as regards all human intercourse. Efforts to make good the omission have been frequent throughout the present century, but volumes by painstaking philologists have, as a rule, been devoid of fruitful suggestions. . . . "Breadth of vision is not conspicuous in modern linguistics," says so well-informed an authority as Jespersen . . . and he attributes this narrow outlook to "the fact that linguists have neglected all problems connected with the valuation of language."

Much of I. A. Richards' work in the study of meaning has also been motivated by the seriousness with which he took (and takes) his job as a teacher. *The Meaning of Meaning* (reflecting the authors' pedagogical concerns) brought to bear on the study of meaning relevant dimensions of psychology, physical science, anthropology, sociology, and philosophy (particularly pragmatism) for the first time. Ogden and Richards set for themselves the task of developing a "science of Symbolism":

> The practical importance of which, even in its present undeveloped form, needs little emphasis. All of the more elaborate forms of social and intellectual life are affected by changes in our attitudes towards, and our use of, words. How words work is commonly regarded as a purely theoretical matter, of little interest to practical persons. . . . The view that language works well enough as it is, can only be held by those who use it merely in such affairs as could be conducted without it. None but those who shut their eyes to the hasty re-adaptation to totally new circumstances which the human race has during the last century been blindly endeavoring to achieve, can pretend that there is no need to examine critically the most important of all the instruments of civilization.

At about the same time, Ludwig Wittgenstein, who had been one of Bertrand Russell's students, extended Russell's work into a philosophical school called "logical positivism." His major work, *Tractatus Logico-Philosophicus,* was published in the United States in 1922. He tried to demonstrate through logical analysis that practically all the traditional problems of philosophy were nonsense, and that most of the disputation in philosophy resulted from a lack of understanding of the "logic of our language."

This point of view was taken up in the 1930's by a group of Polish logicians, including Alfred Tarski and Leon Chwistek. In the United States, Alfred Korzybski was in touch with them, and his own work (which we will discuss presently) was influenced to some extent by the speculations of this group.

In the late 1930's, an international group was formed which was concerned with the possibilities of unifying knowledge through the study of the relation of languages of the various scientific disciplines to each other, as well as the relationship of the language of scientific disciplines to language used in other areas of human activity.

This was an extension of the work of the logical positivists, and of the "Vienna Circle," a group that included Niels Bohr, Rudolf Carnap, John Dewey, Charles Morris, Otto Neurath, and Bertrand Russell. They called themselves "logical empiricists." Charles Morris made an attempt to articulate the foundation for such study in *Signs, Language, and Behavior* (1946).

John Dewey, with Arthur Bentley, pursued a similar search for a unifying perspective in *Knowing and the Known* (1949), which became the basis for what is now called "transactional psychology." In their book, Dewey and Bentley synthesize and extend virtually all preceding modern considerations of problems of meaning from Peirce through Bertrand Russell, and from Ogden and Richards to Charles Morris. The book seems to have been written out of a conviction that traditional "names" (terminology) impede inquiry into and communication about knowledge, and that it would therefore be worth trying some new "firm names for use in connection with the theory of knowledge." As with many other books devoted to semantic concerns, this one is not easily (or widely) read.

At the same time that all the work mentioned above was going on, similar inquiries were being made within conventional academic disciplines. Ernst Cassirer (1874–1945), a German philosopher in the traditional mold, working without apparent awareness of the efforts of those mentioned earlier, published several books devoted to inquiries into meaning. Cassirer's concern with language was primarily epistemological. That is, he was less concerned with language as a medium of communication among men than as man's unique vehicle for carrying knowledge of his world. Cassirer's works, including *Language and Myth* (1946), have been published in English.

Pursuing Cassirer's general philosophical approach in the United States, Susanne Langer wrote *Philosophy in a New Key,* published in 1942. In this important book, Mrs. Langer synthesizes—in substantial detail—modern Western studies of man and his language. In the process, she opens up new directions of inquiry into language as a shaper of thought and perception. She says, for example, at the outset:

> The limits of thought are not so much set from outside, by the fullness or poverty of experiences that meet the mind, as from within, by the power of conception, the wealth of formulative notions with which the mind meets experiences. Most new discoveries are suddenly-seen things that were always there.

She devotes a great deal of attention to the effects of a particular kind of language because of its critical role in man's attempts at generating knowledge: *questions*. She makes the "obvious" point that man's intellectual milestones result not from new answers to old questions, but rather from new questions.

In yet another conventional academic discipline, anthropology, semantics again emerged as a central concern, and, again, apparently without any specific impetus from the efforts being made in other disciplines. What is presently known as *structural linguistics* is to some extent a product of the efforts of anthropologists to describe the structure of languages. Most anthropologists avoided becoming involved in the complexities of semantic problems, but a few, such as Franz Boas and Edward Sapir, felt that such inquiries were indispensable in understanding the culture of a people. Perhaps more than any other group, the anthropological linguists stressed the view that each language, as Sapir put it, represents a different social reality. Although we shall discuss this dimension of language study in a later section, under the heading Metalinguistics, we should mention here (and again) a few of those who advanced the thesis that language *shapes* thought as much as it *expresses* it.

Edward Sapir (1884–1939), an anthropologist at Yale in the latter part of his career, was a pioneer in descriptive linguistics. One of his students, Benjamin Lee Whorf (1897–1941), was a pioneer in metalinguistics. Bronislaw Malinowski (1884–1942), an anthropologist at the University of London, also pioneered in linguistic analysis, which included attention to substance (meaning) as well as to form (structure). Malinowski wrote Supplement I to Ogden and Richards' *Meaning of Meaning.*

Other anthropologists who added, and are adding, to our understanding of the mutual transactions among language, thought, and behavior include Franz Boas, Clyde Kluckhohn, Dorothy Lee, and Edmund Carpenter.

The work of most linguists who have concerned themselves with problems of meaning—from Alexander Bryan Johnson through Peirce, Ogden, and Richards to Carpenter—is almost totally unknown in the schools and among the general public. There is, however, one branch of the study of meaning that has attracted some attention: *general semantics.*

In 1921, Alfred Korzybski, a Polish-born engineer, published *The Manhood of Humanity,* the experience of World War I having provoked him into an attempt at laying the foundations for a "science of man." His focus from the start was the role of language in human affairs, and how it simultaneously enabled man to "bind time" while it blinded him to his own time. In 1933, with the publication of *Science and Sanity,* Korzybski set forth his "science of General Semantics."

In a way, the term *general semantics* is a misnomer. Korzybski preceded the word *semantics* with the word *general* in order to avoid the usual philological and philosophical connotations of semantics. His intention was to combine portions of his General Theory of Time-Binding with studies of language, meaning, and behavior. Thus, he produced the term *general semantics.*

From the outset, general semantics was regarded by Korzybski and his followers as an educational (or perhaps more accurately, a re-educational) discipline. It may be that as a result of this conscious intent, general semantics—of all the various modes of semantic study—has not merely persisted and endured, but has also grown.

This growth has been largely the result of "popularizations" of Korzybski's original work. The most influential of these was written by S. I. Hayakawa, an early student of general semantics. As his doctoral dissertation at the University of Wisconsin, Hayakawa presented a version of Korzybski's approach to the study of language, intending it for use as a textbook in college freshman English courses. In 1941, it was published by Harcourt, Brace, and was subsequently selected by the Book-of-the-Month Club, thus reaching a wide audience. Later revised and retitled *Language in Thought and Action,* it is probably the most frequently used book in both high-school and college courses dealing with semantics. Other "popularizers" of Korzybski's ideas include Stuart Chase (*The Tyranny of Words*), Irving Lee (*Language Habits in Human Affairs*), and Wendell Johnson (*People in Quandaries*). These books restated the substance of Korzybski's methods in ways that enabled most readers to understand them. (In what might be called the "tradition" of written work dealing with semantics, Korzybski's writing, particularly *Science and Sanity,* is difficult to absorb, even for highly educated and sympathetic readers. This fact seems to have qualified Korzybski for inclusion among the least-read and most-criticized writers of the twentieth century.)

In *Science and Sanity,* Korzybski attempted a synthesis of a broad range of "scientific knowledge" (he called it "empirical data"), as well as "nonscientific" knowledge relating to language as man's unique mode of codifying-classifying-evaluating-responding to his perceptions of the world.

Korzybski was convinced that man's "nonscientific, or prescientific, or Aristotelian," use of language increasingly insulated him from reality, and therefore from the prospect of survival. Korzybski attempted to devise a system of "scientific, non-Aristotelian" language strategies intended to keep language users conscious of the degree to which their language corresponded (or did not correspond) to something capable of sense verification.

Even though Korzybski referred to his system as "non-Aristotelian" and explicitly noted Aristotle's contributions to Western thought, many people seem to feel that Korzybski was anti-Aristotelian (which might be used as one example of the kind of "either-or" thinking that Korzybski believed was nonscientific). In fact, Korzybski admired Aristotle, but felt it essential to develop a point of view about language rooted in a different set of goals and assumptions. Addressing himself to the problem of "keeping track of meaning," Aristotle elaborated on a "word game" the Greeks played. The object of the game was to cause an opponent to reverse the position he had originally taken on some matter. The reversal was essentially a shift from disagreement to agreement over something.

Thus, what we now call logic was originally a dialectical game. Aristotle's logic consisted of a series of rules intended to govern the internal consistency of verbal symbols within a specified context. For example, one of the most obvious ways of troubling an opponent in such a word game was to keep changing the intended meaning of a single word during the game. This alone would produce so much confusion that no one could possibly follow what was going on. The rules of logic enable one to "keep track" of meaning—among other things. But note that logical agreement, perhaps most clearly evident in debate today, is a dialectical game played in order to win. This does not mean that it is trivial. Games can be deadly serious. "Game theory," as a matter of fact, is the basis for the development of much of our current military strategy and foreign policy.

What is most important to know about logic is that a game is being played, and that the rules make sense only within the game, and only if they are agreed to by all of the players. In another game, or in the absence of agreement about rules, oddly unpredictable events occur. It should also be noted that the winning of such a game can be starkly sterile. The reason for this resides in the fact that such games are closed systems concerned solely with the manipulation of symbols within the system. There is no attention necessarily paid to correspondence, or lack of correspondence, between the symbols that comprise the currency of the game and anything going on outside the game. Simply put, the game has no necessary connection with reality.

If Korzybski's system has one central point it is that language should bear close correspondence to "reality." This is the substance of sanity. From his point of view, the degree to which language failed to correspond with reality was the degree to which it was not sane. Beyond this, it was Korzybski's view that the kind of language characteristically used in science provided a useful model as to how to go about keeping verbal symbols in close correspondence with observable, verifiable events in reality.

In a way, all scientific activity can be viewed as "semantic verification" in Korzybski's sense. Science, which is an extension and refinement of man's ability to perceive reality, requires that we talk, and hence think, differently about what is going on around us. This kind of talking has always caused a great deal of distress among those who have become enamored of certain words and ideas. The history of science is a chronicle of the unhappy responses that have occurred when someone, somewhere, has pointed out that what everyone had been saying and believing up to that point is nonsense. Galileo with his telescope, Leeuwenhoek with his microscope, and Darwin with his wide-ranging, unaided eyes are just a few examples from literally thousands. Apparently, what we can "see" is not only affected by the language we use, but is in fact determined by our language, and scientists, as never before, seem to be aware of the role that language plays in scientific enterprises. P. W. Bridgman, a Nobel prize-winning physicist, put it this way in *The Way Things Are:*

> The new insights for which I am trying to find a place have mostly been suggested by recent experiences in science which I believe have revolutionary implications not appreciated even by most scientists. Two convictions have been growing upon me—a conviction of the importance of a better understanding of the nature and the limitations of our intellectual tools, and a conviction that there is some fundamental ineptness in the way that all of us handle our minds.

What Bridgman is addressing himself to here is a concern about language, and the way in which it affects how we see, think, and behave. Bridgman's concern was also Einstein's. In *Modern Science and the Nature of Life,* William S. Beck writes:

> Einstein pointed out that the statement "two events some distance apart occur simultaneously" cannot be used to derive any observable fact. Here was the impetus to a

new philosophy whose chief pre-occupation has been with the meaning of language. Since all knowledge must be set forth in language, it is the meaning we give to language which confers upon knowledge its weight and ambiguity. What Einstein was saying was simply that if one wished to understand [an] experiment, one had to commit oneself to the view that the meaning of a statement is strictly related to its verifiability. This conception of the meaning of language had already been voiced by other physicists before Einstein, but it was the monumental work of Einstein that gave these gropings their vast significance for all thought.

Let us consider this question of meaning. I have already mentioned that the great difference between men and beasts is the power to use symbols. Language, of course, is a system of symbols, and it is language, both for its ability to represent ideas and to aid their development, that largely accounts for the intellectual superiority of men over animals. What is curious is the fact that we look so seldom at the phenomenon of language, whose role in the world of affairs has no parallel.

Curious? It gets curiouser and curiouser.

For example, it is interesting to note how many innovations in science can be viewed as being primarily semantic revisions. In other words, the revolution in science is comprised essentially of shifts in metaphor, with the term metaphor here meaning a verbal model for a human perception of reality.

Consider this: When in medicine physicians talked of the "humors" of the body, with some being "good" and others being "bad," one of the most common tactics for doctors to employ in treating their patients was the process called "bleeding." The purpose of bleeding was to let out the "bad humors" that were making the patient ill. With the discovery of the circulation of the blood, the humor theory gradually disappeared from the medical lexicon, whereupon bleeding also vanished as a medical procedure. It might be worth noting, however, that George Washington was bled to death more than one hundred and fifty years after William Harvey's findings made both the theory and metaphor of "humors" obsolete. One cannot resist speculating on how many of our currently accepted theory-metaphors are of an order similar to the once-popular "humors."

In the Bampton lectures at Columbia University in 1952, James B. Conant gave another example:

> To illustrate what seems to me the essence of the new departure in scientific thought, I am going to use an analogy. Let me ask you to consider heat, and to recall that somewhat more than a hundred years ago popular lecturers on science fascinated their audience by demonstrating that heat was a "mode of motion." The notion of a subtle caloric fluid that flowed from hot bodies to cooler ones could be shown to be totally unnecessary; indeed, not only unnecessary but also quite incapable of accounting for a number of experimental results, such as the generation of heat by friction. Therefore, the caloric theory of heat which had been useful in its day was disproved and in its place was firmly established the concept that heat was associated with the motion of particles. Nevertheless, the caloric theory of heat has remained a useful pedagogic device. We still talk of the flow of heat and even set up mathematical expressions to formulate this flow as though there were a caloric fluid. Within a limited range of experimental facts in physics and chemistry, the caloric theory of heat is still the most convenient way of ordering these facts. Note that I said "limited range of facts," for it was the introduction of other experimental situations that destroyed the over-all usefulness of the notion of a caloric fluid. To retain this theory and yet account for all these new facts, one would have to add arbitrary assumption to assumption. On the other hand, when the theory was discarded and heat formulated in terms of the motions of particles, a vast new set of possibilities opened up.

In other words, when the *metaphor* was changed, all kinds of new knowledge was "discovered." Who says words (even in science) are not magic?

Closer attention is being paid to the effects of language in other sciences, too, particularly by those most interested in improving human behavior, or, as was Korzybski, in fostering sanity. Karl Menninger, for example, in his book *The Vital Balance,* describes recent innovations in medicine as follows:

> Diagnosis is changing because we are changing our concepts of illness and disease. . . . But it is very difficult to rid our thinking and our language of the old entity concept of illness. We often speak in figurative terms of "fighting the disease," "facing it," of having a cancer, of suffering from arthritis, or of being afflicted with high blood pressure. This argot reflects the tendency to go on thinking of all disease as a *thing,* a horrid, hateful, alien thing which invades the organism. . . .
>
> But one truth which has to be learned, and re-learned, and re-learned again, because we continually forget it, is that two apparently opposite things can be true. It is sometimes *true* that disease is an invasion; in other instances it is just as true that disease is not an invasion. . . . Illness is in part what the world has done to a victim, but in a larger part it is what the victim has done with his world, and with himself.

And, one might add, what the victim has done with his world and with himself is in no small measure—as Dr. Menninger's comment indicates—determined by the language he uses, and by the way in which he uses it—or lets it use him.

Dr. Menninger goes on to elaborate his concern about the oddly unscientific use of language in the science of medicine. He says:

> What we are objecting to is the inference so easily drawn that the diagnostic labels in common use to describe psychiatric conditions are as definite and constant as those of Tay-Sachs disease. . . . Diagnostic name-calling may be damning. . . . The very word "cancer" is said to kill some patients who would not have succumbed (so quickly) to the malignancy from which they suffer. . . . We disparage labelling of all kinds in psychiatry insofar as these

> labels apply to supposed diseases or conditions of specific etiological determination. We deplore the tendency of psychiatry to retain its old pejorative name-calling functions. Patients who consult us because of their suffering and their distress and their disability have every right to resent being plastered with a damning index tab. Our function is to help these people, not to further afflict them.

A relatively new "field" that might be called "semantic medicine" is developing around the study of *iatrogenic* (doctor-induced) illness. There is accumulating evidence that medical diagnosis can cause a physiological condition. This should come as no surprise in view of the fact that human suggestibility expressed in physiological responses to verbal symbols has long been manifest in what is commonly called hypnosis.

Korzybski's general semantics, then, is an educational system the purpose of which is to train people to use language as scientists do when they are being scientific. This is done through the application of various tactics intended to raise the effects of language to a conscious level, and to keep such awareness relatively constant.

What are some of the specific kinds of awareness Korzybski's system is intended to develop?

First, and probably central to all the others, is the awareness that meaning is not "in" words. Meaning is in people, and whatever meanings words have are assigned or ascribed to them by people. In psychological terminology, this is called projection. To put it simply, we do not "get" meaning from words (or symbols) and "events," we *give* meaning to them. Moreover, people cannot give, assign, or ascribe meanings which they do not already have in their experience. Obviously, a word and its referent that are beyond one's experience are "meaningless." Thus, to talk about what words mean rather than what people mean obscures rather than clarifies the relationship between language and meaning.

A second concept, closely related to the first, is the awareness that words are not what they ostensibly refer to. Or, as it usually is put, "the word is not the thing." This notion seems so "obvious" that it barely seems worth stating. (Bear in mind, though, Alfred North Whitehead's observation that analyzing the obvious has produced some of man's most dramatic intellectual accomplishments.) Apparently, one of man's most primitive traits is to respond to the symbols he invents as if they are whatever it is that he invented them to symbolize. Jean Piaget's studies of the language and thought of children clearly reveal the tendency of children to regard "things" and their names as being virtually the same. But children are not alone in this tendency.

The Old Testament reveals that the name of God was unutterable. In some "primitive" cultures today one's "real name" is kept secret because it is believed that knowing a person's name carries with it the power to control him. If we did not, in our own society, respond to words in this manner, much as "primitive" people do who believe in voodoolike activities, we would not have "dirty" words.

After all, one of the most obvious developments in modern American English is the proliferation of euphemisms, the result of an anxiety and embarrassment about using certain kinds of words. We have in the nuclear-space age all kinds of superstitions about symbols, both verbal and numerical, which indicate that the tendency to confuse symbols with what they stand for is not confined to children and "uncivilized" peoples.

The two kinds of "semantic awarenesses" described above comprise the basis for what can be called consciousness of the process of abstraction. That is, consciousness of the fact that out of a virtually infinite universe of possible things to pay attention to, we abstract only certain portions, and those portions turn out to be the ones for which we have verbal labels or categories. What we abstract, i.e., "see," and how we abstract it, or see it or think about it, is for all practical purposes inseparable from how we talk about it. This is what Einstein, Bridgman, Conant, and Menninger were getting at in the quotes cited earlier.

A third kind of semantic awareness is an extension of the consciousness of abstracting, namely, an awareness of varying levels of abstraction. Words vary in the degree to which they correspond to verifiable referents. Some words are relatively more abstract or general, and some words relatively more concrete or specific. Related to this fact is a fourth kind of semantic awareness, what might be called the "direction of meaning." That is, with increasingly abstract or general words (i.e., those farther removed from operationally verifiable referents) the direction of meaning shifts accordingly from "outside" to "inside." With increasingly concrete or specific words (i.e., those whose referents can be more easily verified operationally) the direction of meaning shifts accordingly from "inside" to "outside."

The conventional semantic terminology for these directions of meaning are *intensional* (internal or inside) and *extensional* (external or outside). Closely bound to these directions of meaning are, of course, different kinds of meaning. The primary semantic distinction made in kinds of meaning is between *connotation* (intensional, subjective, personal meaning) and *denotation* (extensional, objective, social meaning).

Scientific language, which Korzybski used as his model of sane language, is almost exclusively extensional and denotative, or at least tries to be. The language of the mentally ill, most obviously "un-sane," is almost totally intensional and connotative. This is language which does not correspond to anything "out there," and this is, in fact, why the user is mentally ill. Korzybski's concern with keeping conscious "connection" or correspondence between language and externally verifiable referents is, for all practical purposes, paralleled by the process of psychotherapy. In this process, which is largely "just talk," the purpose is to foster closer and more accurate correspondence between the patient's language and externally verifiable meanings. As a semanticist would say, the process of psychotherapy is aimed at shifting the patient's word choices from those having highly intensional connotative meanings to others carrying more denotative meanings. A person suffering from paranoid schizophrenia might use perfectly "correct" English in an unassailably "logical" way, but the problem with his language is that it does not correspond to anything "out there."

And this is the essential basis for the semanticist's contention that sanity is a function of the degree to which language corresponds to things externally verifiable.

A fifth kind of semantic awareness has to do with what might be called the "photographic" effects of language. We live in a universe of constant process. Everything is changing in the physical world around us. We ourselves, physically at least, are always changing. Out of this maelstrom of happenings we abstract certain bits to attend to. We snapshot these bits by naming them. Then we begin responding to the names as if they are the bits we have named, thus obscuring the effects of change. The names we use tend to "fix" that which is named, particularly if the names also carry emotional connotations. For example, physicians warn us not to keep medicine stored in our medicine cabinets much beyond the date for which they were prescribed because their chemistry—along with everything else—keeps changing. What might have been therapeutically valuable at one time may have fatal effects at another—even though its *name* remains the same. There are some semanticists who have suggested that such phrases as "national defense" and "national sovereignty" have been similarly maintained beyond the date for which they were prescribed. What might have been politically therapeutic at one time may prove politically fatal at another.

A variation on the "photographic" effect of language consists of noting how blurred the photograph is. "Blurring" occurs as a result of general class names, rendering distinctions among individual members of the class less visible. One of the most common manifestations of the lack of this kind of semantic awareness can be found in what is called prejudice: A response to an individual is predetermined because the name of the class in which that person is included is prejudged negatively. The most obvious and ordinary remark made in cases of this kind, "They are all alike," makes the point clear.

Other forms of blurring can be found in the most ordinary, everyday statements such as "Teen-agers are irresponsible" or "Boys who wear their hair long are troublemakers" or "Bearded beatniks should be put in the Army." Another kind of blurring is oversimplification. This is commonly a statement of a problem that leaves out critical details. What characterizes most oversimplification is the attribution of single causality to complex problems. Today, for example, the tendency is to attribute any event that is found disconcerting to communist inspiration. The ubiquitous communist is the single cause of anything untoward, from student demonstrations on the West Coast to Negro demonstrations in the South. This tendency to oversimplify has a long history, and it is easier for us to identify it in another time and place. Recognizing it here and now is not only difficult but it also requires courage.

This is perhaps best indicated by your own reaction at this moment. Blaming communism today as the single cause for almost anything that upsets us is so ordinary that we run the risk of incurring hostile responses simply by alluding to it. This is just a current version of the apparently "primitive" need to reduce unwieldy problems to simple dimensions. Today, the communist—*There's* a problem in definition for you! —plays about the same role in the identification of causes of problems as the devil played for a long time in our society.

Oversimplification, of course, has the effect of allowing action to be taken immediately, without one's enduring the burden of undergoing a process of extensional ("out there") verification. Our judicial process represents one attempt by society to minimize oversimplification by insisting upon authentic observations, the verification of facts, and the process of rigorous semantic evaluation (e.g., prosecution-defense dialogue). The problems to which the judicial process addresses itself can, however, be oversimplified; when they are, violence is generally directed against the single "cause" the oversimplification has identified.

Such oversimplification produces both murders of civil rights workers in the South and indiscriminate bombing of "enemy territory" in war. That it serves more to complicate the problem than to solve it seems (at the time at least) to be too romantic an observation to be taken seriously.

This brief list by no means includes all the kinds of awarenesses toward which general semantics addresses itself. One other such problem is a product of the unique features of the English language, such as the unconscious effects of predication. Because of the characteristic word order of English, various kinds of cause-and-effect relationships are assumed that do not in fact exist. In Latin, the warning about this went *"Post hoc ergo propter hoc."* Even in the second decade of the nuclear-space age, it is common to hear all kinds of statements (usually dire) revealing cause-and-effect relationships between "things" connected only by verbs. Perhaps you yourself have heard statements about bad weather being caused by atom bombs, or space flights, or some other "scientific" cause.

One of the verbs semanticists have viewed closely is *to be,* particularly the *is* form. The ordinary verb *is* seems to obscure distinctions between words and referents. The "identity" established between subject and predicate by *is* produces the most common kinds of confusion between words and not-words. For example, in the common statement "It is too hot," the verb *is* makes it "perfectly clear" that *hot* is a "quality" of *It.* Or one might say after a sip of coffee, "It is too sweet." Here, *sweet* is a "quality" of *It.* We will ignore the problem of what the "it" is that is too hot or too sweet. The point is that statements including the word "is" *sound* as if they are about something extensional—"out there"—when they are only about something intensional. "Beauty lies in the eye of the beholder." And sweetness lies in the tongue of the taster, and so on.

Semanticists, following Korzybski, have pursued the making of distinctions among forms and effects of language in the interests of fostering more rational responses to the world. We have devoted so much attention to their work here because it seems to us that, in the linguists' terrain, there are no more relevant inquiries than these.

SEMANTICS IN THE SCHOOLS

What effect on the schools has all of the work in semantics had? For all practical purposes, very little. The teaching of English proceeds in the schools as if none of the ideas we have discussed had ever been thought, written down, and published.

Probably not one English teacher in fifty has ever heard of (much less read) Peirce or Wittgenstein, or Cassirer, or Malinowski, or Sapir. Probably not one English teacher in twenty-five knows of the work of Ogden and Richards or Korzybski. The reasons for this state of affairs are complicated to analyze. One reason probably has to do with the fact that linguistics has been so closely identified with studies in grammar. College courses in linguistics tend to concentrate on developments in grammar, and sometimes on lexicography or on dialect studies. Rarely do they deal with any branch of semantics. In the annual meetings of The National Council of Teachers of English, one can find dozens of workshops and speeches on such topics as Structural Linguistics, Transformational Grammar, and Regional Dialects, but scarcely one on Semantics. In other words, the teaching-of-English "Establishment" does not seem to regard semantics as entirely respectable.* Why this should be so is worth considering. Let us take, as a case in point, general semantics.

From the time that Korzybski's *Science and Sanity* first appeared (1933), it has been viewed with extreme skepticism, especially by members of traditional academic disciplines. Some of the skepticism seems to be simply a product of a misunderstanding of what semantics is getting at. In the recent publication, *Freedom and Discipline in English,* which was prepared by the Commission on English and is supposed to represent the most advanced thinking in the profession, there appears the following paragraph:

> Some consideration must also be given to meaning. Some years ago a number of colleges began to offer courses in "general semantics" which dealt in a one-sided manner with the questions of emotive meaning and reference. Admittedly, a clear comprehension of the function of connotation and denotation is vital in literature and composition, but the prospective teacher must never suppose that language begins and ends there.

* Since this statement was written, one of the authors (CW) has been appointed chairman of the new NCTE Committee for semantics in the schools. There is no cause-and-effect relationship to be assumed.

What can one say of this, except to express the hope that its writer knew better, but chose, for his own reasons, not to reveal what general semantics is about? Nonetheless, there have been substantive criticisms of semantics by practicing semanticists and by well-informed students who are clearly and articulately *not* semanticists themselves.

Their largest single criticism is that semantics is advocated (much as it was by Korzybski) as an educational discipline from which spring all manner of desirable results. However, there appears to be little evidence to substantiate such claims. Advocacy of general semantics, the criticism goes, is still based more on faith than on solid findings from controlled research. This might be called scientific criticism; it meets semantics more or less on its own terms. To some extent, the charge is valid. Some of the early popularizers of semantics (particularly general semantics) were characterized by a fervor and devotion usually exhibited by religious zealots. Moreover, there were practically no studies that could support confidence in the claims of semanticists. However, this situation has drastically changed over the past fifteen years. The work of such men as the late Wendell Johnson, Anatol Rapoport, and Richard Dettering has been both restrained and eminently respectable. In addition, there is a growing body of literature that tends to confirm many of the claims made in behalf of semantics. For example, a particularly important recent inquiry was conducted by Dr. Howard Livingston, of Pace College (New York). His study demonstrated that junior-high-school students who were given instruction in semantics scored significantly higher in critical reading tests than those who had no such instruction.

A somewhat different kind of objection to semantics might be called doctrinal criticism. That is, adherents of "closed systems" of belief commonly object to semantics because they perceive semantics, quite properly, as a kind of antisystem system that takes unchanging absolutes as a prime target for analysis. Semanticists, obviously, analyze the various functions and uses of language. Since one of the most common uses of language is that of control—attempts to affect behavior—this is one of the most common points of semantic thrust.

At the risk of seeming to blur the photograph, we think it worth mentioning that among the most vigorous attacks on semantics are those from the Soviet Union, Senator James Eastland, and the John Birch Society.

It must also be noted, however, that not all people who have strong doctrinal commitments have denied the usefulness of the study of semantics. (See, for example, Mother Margaret Gorman's *General Semantics and Modern Thomism* and Father Daniel Fogarty's *Roots for a New Rhetoric.*)

In general, the educational value conceded to a semantic analysis of language revolves about what is called "the development of critical thinking." The use of semantic strategies—on virtually all grade levels—is seen as enabling students to develop an awareness of various critical distinctions to be made about different kinds of language. Semantics, in other words, is intended to have the effect of liberating one from certain linguistic conventions. And here may be the major reason why semantics has been largely absent from the English curriculum: It is dangerous to conventional beliefs.

Consider, for example, the following question: How many patriotic Americans might have become dedicated Communists had they been born in Russia or China instead of in the United States? Although unanswerable, this question invites interesting speculation, because it is generally assumed that people of political persuasions different from our own have been victimized by indoctrinations from which we have remained free. Our own outlook seems "natural" to us, and we wonder that other men can persist in such false conclusions unless, of course, they are either knaves or fools. Yet, we suspect that for a great many people, perhaps for most, their acceptance of a particular political doctrine is largely attributable to the accident of their birth. Each of us, whether Russian, American, or Chinese, is born into several environments at once, not the least important of which is a semantic environment. Each of us becomes accustomed very early to a "natural" way of talking, and being talked to, about politics. By the time one is old enough to care, his perception of what is either politically right or real is filtered through the recurring words and phrases that form the ritual language of his community's politics. Most men, in time, learn to respond with fervor and obedience to a set of verbal abstractions which they are told and which they believe provides them with an ideological identity. It goes without saying that to those educated to cherish one set of abstractions the different abstractions of other men appear strange or mystifying or threatening.

We take it that it is a mark of an educated man, perhaps even a partial definition of one, that he is not "ideologically interchangeable," which is to say, he is not completely captivated by the political abstractions of the community in which he happened to grow up. Educated persons, however diverse in political opinions, share a common freedom, which is their ability to break through the semantic prejudices of their respective communities.

Let us take a case in point. Below is a segment of an article which appeared in *The New York Times* on September 27, 1962. Assuming that he had read it in his own press, what would an educated Russian or Chinese have made of it?

> President Kennedy and the Government of the United States as a whole were reviled today at a public meeting held in Peking to welcome political representatives of South Vietnam's Communist guerillas.
>
> Kuo Mo-Jo, chairman of the China Peace Committee, declared at the meeting, which was attended by Marshal Chen Yi, the Chinese Foreign Minister, that President Kennedy "surpassed Hitler and Tojo in savagery and tyranny."
>
> United States "imperialism," he said, is the "sworn enemy of peace and the most ferocious enemy of people all over the world."
>
> "United States imperialism is United States imperialism. Kennedy is Kennedy. Cholera bacteria is cholera bacteria," he went on. . . .
>
> "There are countless pieces of evidence that show we should cherish no illusions about imperialism, especially United States imperialism, and that we can only wage a

head-on and unremitting struggle against it, tooth for tooth and eye for eye."

Perhaps the first observation an educated Russian or Chinese would make is that Kuo Mo-Jo's statements are almost hysterically one-sided. Even if he has been kept ignorant of any United States actions that might be characterized as peaceful, he will probably assume that no government can be so totally bad as Kuo Mo-Jo has pictured the United States, nor as totally good as Kuo Mo-Jo has implied his own government is. Black-and-white characterizations are admissible in a morality play, but rarely, if ever, do governments make vivid symbols of virtue and vice.

Our Russian or Chinese reader might also be struck by the belligerent language of the chairman of a "peace committee": ". . . we can only wage a head-on and unremitting struggle against [United States imperialism], tooth for tooth and eye for eye." Whatever else might be said about such talk, it is not peaceful—in any language. A careful reader would not let the contradiction go unnoticed. Perhaps our foreign reader has not previously read George Orwell. But even if he has not, he might think to himself that it is a curious "peace" committee indeed whose chairman swears unremitting hostility to an opposing political force.

If our reader has some reliable information about recent political history, he will probably think, too, that Kuo Mo-Jo's comparison of Kennedy to Hitler and Tojo is somewhat extreme. Even if the reader disapproves fully of Kennedy's positions on Berlin, Cuba, South Vietnam, and Formosa, he is not likely to be persuaded that such positions, however threatening, surpass in savagery and tyranny the actions of Hitler and Tojo. An educated Russian knows too much about Hitler to be taken in by that; an educated Chinese, too much about Tojo.

Our reader would understand also that a word like "imperialism" has almost no descriptive value. It is almost always used as an epithet applied to someone else's country, never to one's own. He suspects that government leaders talk of "protecting national security" when they advocate doing that which is called "imperialism" when done by another nation.

Finally, he would perhaps wonder what in the world Kuo Mo-Jo means in saying, "United States imperalism is United States imperialism. Kennedy is Kennedy. Cholera bacteria is cholera bacteria." Our reader would recognize here what seems to be a classic instance of the confusion of words with the things words describe. Does Kuo Mo-Jo think that the words "United States imperialism" are identical with the actions the term is intended to describe? Our reader may well wonder to what absurdities such a confusion might lead. Does Kuo Mo-Jo think Mao Tse-tung is beneficent because he is "Mao Tse-tung"? that Marxism is correct because it is "Marxism"? that cholera bacteria is called "cholera bacteria" because it is so deadly? Upon reading Kuo Mo-Jo's statements, our educated Russian or Chinese would have good cause to question the wisdom if not the motives of their author. Certainly, the latter's words are not likely to inflame the passions of one who knows how to read.

Of course, to an American reader, well educated or not, Kuo Mo-Jo presents no problem. The language of Communists has been extensively analyzed by American politicians and reporters. As a consequence, most Americans are alert to the dogmatisms, oversimplifications, and rhetorical excesses of communists. But how well does an American deal with the language of his own leaders? On the same day on which Kuo Mo-Jo's statements were published in *The New York Times,* there appeared another article, not many columns away, which reported the views of several congressmen concerning the situation in Cuba. An excerpt from this article follows:

> Five Republicans, led by Representative John J. Rhodes of Arizona, chairman of a special policy subcommittee, called for an explicit reaffirmation of the Monroe Doctrine. The original statement by President James Monroe in 1823 warned that European intervention in Western Hemisphere affairs was a danger to United States security.
>
> The House Republican whip, Leslie C. Arends of Illinois, said:
>
> "It is apparent that this Administration lacks a cohesive sound plan as to ways and means to deal with the despot's

heel which has not only set up headquarters 90 miles from our shore but poses a potential military threat."

Representative Clarence Brown, Republican of Ohio, said:

"In the past we have used troops in Latin America and were called 'Yankee imperialists,' but we had the respect of Latin America and the rest of the world, too, for that matter.

"If Teddy Roosevelt had been in power, the Marines would have been in, and the beard would have been shaved off the first week."

What one has granted to the educated Russian or Chinese, one must unhesitatingly grant to the educated American. Even if he passes over the disingenuousness of the *Times'* explanation of the Monroe Doctrine, it is simply not possible that a careful reader will fail to note how intensionally oriented are the brief statements of Messrs. Brown and Arends, including the ludicrous image of a despot's heel setting up headquarters in Havana. However, perhaps the most significant insight that would come from an analysis of these statements is the similarity in their doctrinaire tone to those of Kuo Mo-Jo.

Our assumption is that educated persons would perceive that we have here illustrations of how words may serve as the bricks from which walls of hostility and misunderstanding are built. The masons are political leaders who through design or ignorance are helping to keep different peoples from seeing each other, from seeing their common interests, from seeing even their common dangers. How are such walls to be broken down? As we have intimated, they are at least pierced by those who have been educated to analyze language in a critical and detached manner. When we referred to an "educated" Russian or Chinese or American, we were, of course, thinking of a person who possessed such competency, one who knows something about the uses of language, the levels of abstraction at which language operates, its relation to what we call reality; in other words, the substance of what is called semantics.

The systematic teaching and practice of such a complex of competencies would probably be more widespread if it were not for the fact that they are essentially "subversive" activities from the point of view of Kuo Mo-Jo and Messrs. Brown and Arends. For there is probably no clearer act of "subversion" than that of a man in the process of discovering that the language of his leaders is nonsensical or one-sided. A Chinese who recognizes these characteristics in Kuo Mo-Jo's statements is a potentially "dangerous" man. He is, for example, probably not an avid Communist. He is certainly unlikely to be an aggressive and therefore entirely useful participant in the Cold War. An American who identifies in Representative Brown's statement similar tendencies is likewise potentially "dangerous."

Such people are dangerous because they are not easily enlisted on the side of one ideology or another; and when they are, they insist on looking beyond mere name-calling and sterile slogans to the actions of those who are supposed to provide an ideology with its reality. In his *May Man Prevail?* Erich Fromm gives us an example of a man (himself) in the process of doing just that:

> The Russians believe that they represent socialism because they talk in terms of Marxist ideology, and they do not recognize how similar their system is to the most developed form of capitalism. We in the West believe that we represent the system of individualism, private initiative, and humanistic ethics, because we hold on to *our* ideology, and we do not see that our institutions have, in fact, in many ways become more and more similar to the hated system of communism.

What would the world look like if it were populated by men like Fromm? What would be the tone of debates in the United Nations? What would Kuo Mo-Jo talk about? Would he be forced to admit that the Chinese government itself has been "imperialistic"? Would he say that Kennedy frequently acted out of genuine fear of communist aggression? And what kinds of statements would Representative Brown make? Would he say that the United States has acted aggressively before and intends to act so again, even though we are despised for it?

Of course, political leaders rely heavily on the continuing irrelevance of such speculations as these. Educational systems are largely designed to enjoin citizens, within varying but harmless limits of objectivity, to accept the verbal maps drawn by political leaders. When educational processes do not do this, they usually become suspect. Kuo Mo-Jo depends on an educational process that will insure that citizens "think Chinese." Representative Brown depends on an educational process that will insure that citizens "think American." Semantics, of course, is dangerous to both.

And yet, if anyone is to take seriously the substance of John W. Gardner's remarks quoted at the beginning of Part II of this book, semantics would have to play an important role in education. Some teachers have begun to move in that direction.

We have already mentioned Hayakawa's *Language in Thought and Action,* which is used in many colleges and some high schools. Another book sometimes used in the schools is Catherine Minteer's *Words and What They Do to You.* But this book is intended more as a guide for teachers than as a textbook to be put into the hands of students. The same is true of *Language Power for Youth,* edited by Cleveland Thomas, which is a compendium of descriptions, largely by teachers of English in high school, of relatively episodic studies of semantics.

Although the study of semantics on all grade levels below college is still what might be called a fugitive enterprise, we can provide a few descriptions of semantic studies in the classroom.

In general, semantic study has as its purpose the development of a perspective on certain language habits and their effects in order to produce perceptible changes in behavior. That is, students who are learning semantic processes (as compared with learning semantic terms only) are expected to speak, evaluate, and behave more rationally, reasonably, humanely, scientifically, and so on. This being the case, teachers have tried to involve students on as personal a level as possible. Toward this end, one teacher in Long Island started his class by simply asking the students whether they had ever been involved in a serious "misunderstanding." After some oral attempts at describing such episodes, the students were asked to write "case histories" of the events. The most suitable of these were edited and duplicated for distribution to the class. Each case was used as a problem, and inquiries were conducted into the cases for the purpose of determining the sources of misunderstanding. The teacher launched the inquiry by asking the seemingly simple question, "What's the problem here?" The teaching strategy throughout was on *educing* responses from the students.

One of the hazards of the case-study approach is that there can be an overabundance of examples of the kinds of semantic confusion that are under study. Nonetheless, in this instance, the students were able to identify at least four different kinds of semantic blocks to communication, chief among which was "bypassing." As explained by one student, "Bypassing is what happens when the speaker assumes that his listener will always assign the same meanings to terms that he [the speaker] assigns to them." Equipped with this principle, the student was able to identify in the local newspaper on a single day three instances of "bypassing."

Another teacher had his students use relevant political problems as cases. The students chose to analyze not only contemporary examples of obstructed communication, but historical ones as well. In this instance, students were able to identify, and state in their own language, such semantic problems as "blurring," confusion of levels of abstraction, and identification of words with things. Both of the following cases were discovered by students themselves, and subsequently analyzed by them:

1. (from *Esquire*)

> Ahmad told me another story of military service, involving friends. "Each year in the army they have these maneuvers," he said. "So these friends of mine are in maneuvers with guns in the desert and they have orders: shoot to kill. Now one of them was Ibrahim, my friend.

Ibrahim goes to this outpost in the dark. They make him stop and ask him for the password. But he has forgotten the password. So they say, 'He must be the enemy.' "

I asked if this took place in wartime. "No, no, maneuvers. My friend Ibrahim say, 'Look, I forget. I *did* know but now I forget the password but you know me, anyway, you know it's Ibrahim.' And he's right; they do know it was Ibrahim. . . . But since he cannot say the password they shot him."

"Shot him? Dead?"

"Dead," said my host with melancholy satisfaction. "Oh, they were sorry, very sorry, because they knew it was Ibrahim, but you see, *he did not know the password,* and while he was dying in the tent they took him to, he said it was all right. They were right to kill him."

2. (from ***The New York Times***)

"CITIZEN EDUCATION" IS SOCIAL STUDIES AGAIN

Albany, November 18—The Board of Regents today went back to the term "social studies" to describe elementary- and secondary-school courses in geography, history, government and economics.

The Regents had dropped "social studies" in favor of "citizen education" in 1950 because some members of the board at the time believed that the original phrase smacked of socialism.

In reversing themselves today, the Regents noted that "social studies" described the subject matter more accurately, that it had been in use for more than fifty years and that it was accepted by colleges and professional groups.

A wide range of literary works has been used as the material for semantic inquiry. Short stories, such as "The Lottery" and "After You, My Dear Alphonse," by Shirley Jackson, have seemed especially suitable for providing insight into ritualistic responses, particularly to black and white symbolism. Virtually any of the plays by Shakespeare used in high school (even in their bowdlerized form) can also be used, and on rare occasions have been, as the basis of a semantic inquiry. One teacher had his students treat *Julius Caesar* and *Macbeth* as "case histories" —replete with fatal misunderstandings—of semantic problems of various kinds. *Othello* and *King Lear* have also proven to be rich sources of descriptions of human beings in trouble, frequently as a result of failing to make the kinds of language distinctions semantics insists upon. (For a number of reasons, English teachers could do much worse than to approach Shakespeare semantically!)

"Documentary" material has also been used to help students learn important semantic strategies. A bridge of such material was arranged by one teacher—starting with Cotton Mather's description of his observation of the effects of witches upon young girls and moving to contemporary descriptions of a similar order; for example, Robert Welch's descriptions of Dwight Eisenhower and Earl Warren.

This same teacher required his students to do a semantic analysis of certain television programs that occupy prime time (and the attention of his students). He even went so far as to invite several students to do a semantic analysis of a James Bond movie, his assumption being that this is more educative than merely deploring the fact that students spend so much time watching James Bond movies. Indeed, it would seem obvious that we should be using these materials for semantic analysis *because* students spend so much time with them.

These brief descriptions of semantics in the schools do not, unfortunately, suggest the full range of possibilities. The problem is, of course, that too few teachers have allowed their students to engage in semantic inquiries. Since what semanticists try to do is foster more rational behavior by applying scientific procedures of inquiry and verification to ordinary language, the authors feel that the neglect of semantics in the English class is a tragedy.

CHAPTER 7

Lexicography and Dialect Geography

LEXICOGRAPHY AND THE LINGUISTS

As S. I. Hayakawa has put it, dictionaries are history books, not law books. This is the basic concept that linguistics brings to lexicography. It is a point of view accepted by almost all professional students of language, and it has the precedence of history and the demands of science to support it. In this view, the function of a lexicographer is to record as accurately as his procedures and energy allow the actual usage of speakers and writers of a language. He describes, in other words, how as a matter of fact and public record words are used at a given time in the history of a people and their language.

Incredible as it sounds, there are many otherwise sensible people who not only object to this point of view, but who are prepared to fight about it. In 1961, with the publication of *Webster's Third New International Dictionary,* such people became distressingly noticeable, and from all quarters, both predictable and unsuspected. In general, their assaults were directed against Philip B. Gove, under whose editorial direction *Webster's Third* was compiled. Articles, reviews, and editorials appeared, for example, in *The New Yorker, Life, Time, The Atlantic,* and *The New York Times.* The major charge appeared to be that Gove and his associates had betrayed a trust. The function of a lexicographer, the complaints asserted, is *not* to report on the language, but to evaluate it, judge it, make recommendations about it, and in general behave as a kind of Chief Justice of English. The most common characteristic of these attacks, in addition to their violence and abundance, was their aggressive ignorance of linguistic science. What had happened, simply, was this: Under Gove's direction, *Webster's Third* appeared as the first modern dictionary to result from the rigorous application of descriptive linguistics to lexicography. People who otherwise could not have cared less about linguistics suddenly were aroused. More particularly, what was aroused were the moralistic and prescientific attitudes about language that are so pervasive, especially among those of the intellectual and educated class.

We have remarked earlier on the fact that many people find it extremely difficult to function without the illusion of certainty. We have also remarked that uncertainty and tentativeness are fundamental attitudes of science. Thus, issues developed: Could we no longer rely on dictionaries to tell us what is right? Did we have to suffer the indignity of dictionaries that told us only the truth? Were all standards to be washed away in the waves of science? Where would we turn for arbitration on language matters? In short, *Webster's Third* was viewed as a kind of linguistic Kinsey Report, condemned because its authors felt obliged to describe human behavior rather than dictate its course.

Where do dictionaries come from anyway? What are they supposed to do? How did it all start?

As with most stories about specific areas of human behavior, the story of lexicography is long and complicated. The description provided in an earlier chapter on the evolution of grammar parallels that for lexicography with but few variations. One of these parallels is found in the desire of the eighteenth-century English "middle class" to achieve social respectability through language. The pressures generated by this group affected the publication of dictionaries, as well as of grammar books. However, prior to these conditions, in the late fifteenth and early sixteenth centuries, and for reasons of a more "realistic" nature, there had developed a demand for foreign-language dictionaries. The combination of Latin's giving way as an international language and the increase in international trade (which increased the need for multilingual abilities), made inevitable the production of such books. The earliest of these included English-Welsh, English-Spanish, and Italian-English dictionaries. These word collections were not, however, called "dictionaries" at this early date. Their format consisted largely of simple columns of word equivalents, modeled after the still earlier "glosses" that were in use when Latin was the international language of all medieval Europe. In these early beginnings of the dictionary, a column of difficult Latin terms was matched by a column of easier—more common—ones. It is interesting to note that the earliest versions of written English we have may be found in glosses (from the Anglo-Saxon period) in which Latin terms were matched with English (Anglo-Saxon) terms.

The present moralistic attitudes toward usage may well have their roots in the late sixteenth century when a form of intellectual posturing became relatively common in literary English. The reading of Greek and Latin gave small-minded pedants an opportunity to lard their writing with polysyllabic Latin and Greek words. This form of linguistic one-upmanship is not uncommon today, and is sometimes even encouraged by teachers of English in "composition."

In any event, the "English" which was produced by such posturing was virtually unreadable to anyone who didn't spend a great deal of time and effort trying to gain familiarity with Latin and Greek. One way to bypass the problem was to have a gloss that "translated" these private words into ordinary English. It was on such a reference work that the term *dictionary* first appeared: *The English Dictionary,* subtitled *An Interpretater of Hard Words,* published in 1623. There were similar compilations, before and after, devoted to the same purpose, but none were called dictionaries.

Prior to the middle of the eighteenth century, the production of "hard-word" books diminished, possibly because the fad of classical pedantry had ended. There followed word books that focused largely on literary usage. The literary style characteristic of eighteenth-century England was simple and clear. Uncluttered syntax and unobtrusive vocabulary combined to form a standard which the literary world felt should be preserved.

In 1721, Nathaniel Bailey produced what is generally regarded as the first English language dictionary, intended partly to preserve the language traditions of England's best contemporary writers. His work was entitled *An Universal Etymological English Dictionary.* Bailey, however, was a man of more than slight scientific orientation, and his dictionary was prepared in a way quite congenial to the spirit of modern linguistics. For example, it included (1) etymology, (2) a careful attention to modern usage, (3) syllabification, (4) pronunciation, (5) contextual meanings (word usage illustrated by quotations), and (6) illustrations. Bailey, virtually by himself, established the ground rules for lexicography as it is even now practiced. He has been called one of the few geniuses that lexicography has produced.

What about Dr. Johnson? Mostly, he "stole" from Bailey. Lexicographers, it has been observed by one lexicographer, are professional thieves. In other words, it is a conventional practice for the makers of a new dictionary to "borrow" heavily from existing dictionaries. (One of the several remarkable achievements of *Webster's Third* is that its editors revised almost all of the definitions that appeared in *Webster's Second.*)

Samuel Johnson's *Dictionary,* published in 1755, was largely an extension of Bailey's work, although with some notable differences. One difference resulted from the fact that Johnson wrote more colorfully than Bailey. Some of Johnson's definitions are memorable; are, in fact, small literary gems. A second difference is that Johnson was less scientific than Bailey. If Bailey is the father of lexicographers, Johnson is the father of all the self-appointed protectors of the "purity" of English. As he set out to purify English, Johnson was probably influenced by such naive enterprises as the French Academy (established for the preservation of the "purity" of French). Johnson provided a lexicographic focus for those who needed to have the illusion of certainty and stability. That is, there were those who felt it important to believe not only that "there will always be an English language" but also that it will always be exactly as it is *now* (i.e., at the time *they* are using it). While Johnson did not deny that language changes, he did not leave any doubt that he was against its doing so, and his dictionary represents, in a way, his protest. Johnson's always unhesitating, mostly moralistic, and frequently arbitrary judgments about words, combined with the pitiful dependence on "authority" of the middle class, are probably the precedents for the notion that the dictionary is the "supreme authority" as to what is and what is not correct in English usage. Various dictionaries followed Johnson's in the eighteenth century, but in England, right up to this century, the word *dictionary* meant Johnson's *Dictionary*. Unfortunately, Bailey's rigorous procedures for making judgments about words were not always duplicated by dictionary makers—including Johnson. Many of them were what might be called armchair classifiers who had neither the inclination nor training to engage in active inquiry. When competently practiced, lexicography is a demanding and formidable task. It involves engaging in a wide-ranging and intensive search for words, including attempts to catalogue their use in a variety of contexts, spoken as well as written. Moreover, the lexicographer is condemned to chronic frustration: All his attempts to describe words are tentative and approximate. Not only is a living language constantly changing but also no word ever has identical meanings in any two different contexts. A moment's reflection on such matters as tone in language will reveal that there are few, if any, exact synonyms within a language (much less "exact translations" of words from one to another language).

The first formal attempt at advancing lexicography through linguistic science was launched in London in 1858 by the Philological Society. Over the next seventy years, the Society collected millions of entries from printed material of every kind over a wide span of history. Indeed, no other dictionary had ever recorded any language with such detailed historical documentation or such sensitive distinctions among the various senses in which words are used. The result of this effort was, of course, *A New English Dictionary on Historical Principles* (*NED*), published by the Oxford University Press in 1928; and which ran to 15,487 quarto pages, nearly half a million words, and more than a million and a half illustrative quotations. In 1933, it was reissued under its present title, *The Oxford English Dictionary* (*OED*). Every speaker and writer of English should at some time in his life inspect this remarkable work. Almost by itself it provides all the data needed to formulate the most important generalizations about the English language. Even today, it has no rival, either in England or America.

The earliest American dictionaries were intended almost exclusively for use in the schools. They were based on Johnson's *Dictionary,* which probably accounts in part for many of the eighteenth-century English attitudes toward language still clung to by twentieth-century Americans.

The earliest significant date in American lexicography is 1828, the year in which Noah Webster's *An American Dictionary of the English Language* (two volumes) appeared. Webster was rather more like Johnson than Bailey in his lexicographic endeavors. Nonetheless, Webster broke precedent by expressing an unmistakable bias toward native American-English. He took great pains to emphasize the differences between the two "Englishes." In a way, American-English was seen by Webster as symbolizing unique American virtues and values—notably simplicity and freedom from affectation. Webster's spellings, definitions, and contextual illustrations were all distinctly American. Most of our current "American" spellings, as distinct from British spellings, are a result of Webster's simplifications. More important for the development of lexicography was his insistence on sharp, cogent, and clear definitions.

It goes without saying that throughout the history of lexicography—from Bailey to Funk and Wagnalls—innovations in lexicography have been important only to lexicographers. Most people are accustomed to saying "Look it up in the dictionary" with an unconscious emphasis on *the,* and an equally unconscious assumption that the differences among dictionaries are negligible. One might even say that lexicography is a genteel and unobtrusive pursuit, of interest only to professional lexicographers. That is, it was until 1961!

Perhaps, the decade of the sixties in the United States will someday be seen as one in which a great number of American prejudices—social, political, economic, and linguistic—were confronted with truths that precipitated "revolutions" of several kinds. For example, Negro suffrage in the South; the election of a Catholic President; the enactment of Medicare legislation; and the appearance of a dictionary resulting explicitly from scientific lexicography.

In any case, the basic assumptions of modern lexicography may be stated as follows:

1. All languages are systems of human conventions, not systems of natural laws.

2. Each language is unique in its pronunciation, grammar, and vocabulary. It cannot be described in terms of any other language, or even in terms of its own past.

3. All living languages are in a continual process of change. A "rule" about a language has no status unless it is a generalization about contemporary practice.

4. The function of a dictionary is to provide an accurate and comprehensive record of current usage at a given point in history.

5. It is not the function of the lexicographer to prescribe ways in which language should be used.

6. In the interests of accuracy, the lexicographer should give an indication of the status, among educated people, of certain words and expressions.

7. The problems of identifying the "educated" are almost as complex as those of defining words. This is especially true when dealing with a pluralistic society and a growing, wide-ranging language.

8. The more representative the sources from which meanings are gathered, the more accurate will be the dictionary.

Allow us to conclude by making the simple observation that if these assumptions constitute sabotage of our language, their victim is merely a tradition of linguistic prejudice and unscientific scholarship.

DIALECT GEOGRAPHY AND THE LINGUISTS

Like lexicography, the discipline of dialect geography is best conducted in quiet, noncontroversial circumstances. Unlike lexicography, however, linguistic geography has apparently not yet been "discovered" by the popular press, which doubtless would disapprove of it since its basic assumptions derive from descriptive linguistics.

Dialect geography may be defined as the attempt to describe and catalogue the characteristics of various regional dialects. The main contributions of dialect geographers are threefold. First, they have developed a precise, technical vocabulary with which to talk about the varieties of language. Second, they have evolved systematic procedures for obtaining the kinds of data they seek. And, third, they have accumulated a vast amount of information, although there is still much that is not yet known.

1. Terminology. Obviously, there is no term more basic to dialect geography than the word *language*. To the layman, there would seem to be no difficulty in defining language. A language is—well, a language. Like French, Russian, or German. A moment's reflection reveals, however, that the matter is not so simple. For instance, German and Yiddish are usually thought of as two different languages; yet, those who speak one claim to be able to "understand" those who speak the other. Perhaps not very well, but how much similarity do two languages have to have before we say that they are one, not two? Or consider the case of "English." If a man from Bogalusa, Louisiana, claims that he does not "understand" a man from Glasgow, Scotland, is it reasonable to say that both men speak the same language? The dialect geographer is painfully aware of these complexities. He begins by recognizing the obvious fact that no two people speak exactly alike (as proven by the oscillograph). In other words, each individual speaks his own "language." The name given to this private language is *idiolect.* But it is also obvious that the idiolects of some people have great similarities in pronunciation, vocabulary, and grammar. People whose idiolects closely resemble each other are therefore said to be members of the same *speech community.* There are, of course, many kinds of speech communities. For example, you and your family constitute a speech community on the basis of the fact that your characteristic pronunciations, grammar, and vocabulary are probably quite similar. You and other members of your profession form still another kind of speech community, based largely on the fact that your vocabularies are so much alike. When a speech community exists on the basis of geography—that is, when speakers of a particular geographic region exhibit similar idiolects, their particular speech habits are said to constitute a *dialect.* Note at once that the term dialect is not used in any derogatory sense. It is a descriptive and technical term. Note too that the term is an abstraction that refers to a bundle of similar idiolects, characterized by their location in a particular geographic region. In the same way, a *language* is an abstraction that refers to a bundle of similar dialects and speech communities. Linguists usually invoke the criterion of mutual intelligibility to determine if two dialects are part of the same language. This method of classification is rigorous enough to solve most problems, although not all. In other words, in the case of a "language" such as English, the variations among dialects can be so great that mutual intelligibility between certain pairs is extremely hard to show. Nonetheless, a language may be viewed as a composite of overlapping dialects, which are, in turn, composites of overlapping idiolects.

As you would expect, dialect geographers do not consider such questions as: Which dialects are better than others? Since there is no *linguistic* basis for making such judgments, linguists are content to leave these questions to literary critics and philosophers. The point is that although the speakers of one dialect may be barely intelligible to you such people have no difficulty in understanding one another. On the other hand, your own speech may be barely intelligible to them.

2. Methods of Inquiry. In general, there are three kinds of differences among dialects: pronunciation, grammar, and vocabulary. Collecting data about them is an exacting and time-consuming enterprise. The general outlines of this process of inquiry are described in the passage below, taken from *Dialects, U.S.A.*, by Jean Malmstrom and Annabel Ashley:

The Systematic Methods of Linguistic Geography.

When the speech of any particular region is analyzed, the region's economic and cultural history and its geography must first be studied. In the light of this study, a set of communities within the region is selected for thorough investigation. These communities are ones which have played an important part in the history of the region. Perhaps they were early permanent settlements or were located on vital trade or migration routes. Or perhaps they were, or are, urban centers of culture and industry. Contrariwise, they might have been relatively isolated communities and therefore may have preserved older forms of the local language. Or perhaps they have a large foreign population and thus show the effect of foreign language borrowings. At any rate, these representative communities are carefully chosen to form a network which will give an adequate cross section of the region's known historical, cultural, economic, and geographic composition.

Next, individuals within each community are selected to furnish the needed information about the speech of the region. These individuals are chosen because they will fully represent the population of the community. They must range from old to young, from high to low on the social and economic scale, and from college to less than eighth grade education. In the records of the Linguistic Atlas of the United States, these informants are classified as follows:

I. Old-fashioned, rustic speakers of eighth grade education.

II. Younger, more modern speakers of high school education.

III. Cultured speakers of college education.

These persons, technically called "informants," are then interviewed by a trained interviewer called a "field worker," who uses a questionnaire designed to bring out words and phrases which will give regional information on pronunciation, vocabulary, and grammar. The items on the questionnaire are chosen for three main reasons: 1) because they refer to common things which will be known to most of the people of the region, 2) because they are easy to introduce into a friendly conversation, and 3) because they are known to have regional or social variants. Such items usually concern ordinary everyday life within the intimate circle of the family and the community. For example, groups of items cluster around the weather, the home, food, clothing, and the farm with its animals, crops, vehicles, and utensils. Interspersed among such vocabulary groups are others more directly concerned with grammar—on verb forms and verb phrases, on pronouns, adverbs, and prepositions.

The interview may last anywhere from six to twenty hours and is carried on in as conversational a way as possible. Using a special phonetic alphabet which can record more than four hundred differences in vowel sounds alone, the field worker writes down what the informant says about each item and how he pronounces it. The items are listed on sheets of paper called "work sheets," which are bound into notebooks. Some field workers have used tape and disc recorders to record their interviews.

Since interviewing of this sort is very expensive and time-consuming, some of the American linguistic geographers have used another method to collect dialect information. This method is the postal check list. In this method a questionnaire is sent out by mail to be filled in and returned by an informant. In this way a much larger sampling of speakers can be made, even though their

> responses are usually less full and detailed than those gathered by the interview method. Differences in pronunciation are difficult to discover by this method. However, comparisons show that the check list responses substantially corroborate the findings of the field workers.

One of the most widely used systems for dealing with the data collected by these procedures is to construct maps which depict the geographic boundaries of certain pronunciations, word meanings, and grammatical features. For example, a dialect geographer who finds that a word is used only in a certain region, draws a line (called an *isogloss*) that represents the geographic boundaries of the word. Similar maps may be constructed to depict the geographic boundaries of pronunciation and grammatical features.

3. Accumulated knowledge. Without question, the most substantial record of the dialect variations of the United States is charted, catalogued, and depicted in what is called *The Linguistic Atlas of the United States.* The proposal for this mammoth undertaking was first made in 1929, and work on the *Atlas* is still going on. The first *Atlas,* covering New England, was begun under the general direction of Professor Hans Kurath. Field interviewing began in 1931 and was completed in 1933. Between 1939 and 1943, six large volumes of 734 maps were published, representing *The Linguistic Atlas of New England.* Under the direction of Kurath, Albert H. Marckwardt, Harold Allen, and others, work has been undertaken, at one time or another, to produce *Atlases* of the Middle Atlantic and South Atlantic states, the North Central states, the Upper Midwest, the Rocky Mountain states, the Pacific Coast, and the Inland South.

Perhaps the single most important idea emerging from research in dialect geography is Professor Kurath's conception of the three major dialect areas of the eastern United States. Kurath has divided this region into Northern, Midland, and Southern dialect areas. Research has pointed to the fact that these areas extend from east to west across the continent.

In general, these findings make obsolete the widely held

notion of a "general American" dialect, presumed to extend from New Jersey through the Middle West and on to the Pacific Coast. Research indicates that even such a conception as a "Midwest" dialect is a vast oversimplification. Also, there is little evidence to support the notion that dialect groupings are reflected by state boundaries. Dialects apparently operate without any respect for such political conceptions as state lines.

LEXICOGRAPHY AND DIALECT GEOGRAPHY IN THE SCHOOLS

Typically, lexicography and dialect geography, when they are dealt with at all in the classroom, are "presented" as a two- or three-week "unit." The purpose of such a unit is "to teach the students how to use the dictionary" or "to provide students with an understanding of the richness and variety of their language." In a few cases, such purposes are achieved, but almost always at the expense of serious inquiry into the most important questions posed by these disciplines. In most cases, the purposes of the units are not achieved; that is, skills do not improve and attitudes remain unchanged. However, teachers of English who are concerned with linguistics as a process have begun to evolve procedures for teaching lexicography and dialect geography that are designed to achieve not only traditional purposes but also others of equal importance.

Below, we have described two such procedures, taken directly from the work of particular classrooms. You will note that in each case the teacher is concerned that the students *act* as linguists do. You will note too that neither of the procedures described can be "presented" in a two- or three-week unit. Both require sustained inquiry, which may last an entire term.

Lexicography. In a New York high school, tenth-grade students were faced with the challenge of compiling a "teen-age dictionary." According to their teacher, who unilaterally posed the problem for them, a teen-age dictionary is one that includes words and phrases that are unique to the language of teenagers. The notion appealed to the students at once, although they had no idea in what complicated directions their enthusiasm would take them. What probably attracted the students most was their certainty, quite accurate, that they were "authorities" on teen-age language, or were, in any case, more knowledgeable on the subject than their teacher. It is worth noting that too often students are not permitted to draw on their own considerable experience with English as a legitimate source of knowledge about language. This classroom was, quite obviously, different—a fact that the teacher stressed.

The initial task of the students was to decide what kind of dictionary they wanted to make. At first, most of the students were befuddled by the problem. "What do you mean—What *kind* of dictionary?" some asked. "There *is* only one kind—a dictionary!" Their teacher was prepared for the confusion, since he knew that most Americans believe that all dictionaries are almost identical, and that one is about as good as another. He therefore presented the students with the following two passages:

> The proper function of a dictionary is to safeguard our language from corruption. People depend on dictionaries to set standards of good usage. A good dictionary will not dignify coarse, vulgar, or substandard language by including it in its pages, unless, of course, such language is clearly labeled as coarse, vulgar, or substandard. The lexicographer must decide how to answer the question: What is acceptable language? That question must always be settled by consulting the works of the best writers and soliciting the advice of the truly educated and refined. It would be a perversion of the concept of democracy to use the speech of the common man as a guide to what is right. The common man knows that his speech is deficient. He turns to a dictionary to learn how he *ought* to speak, not how he *does*.

> The proper function of a dictionary is to record, without bias, the way language is being used at a particular time in history. If most people use the word "disinterested" as a synonym for "uninterested," then the lexicographer must record that usage as "standard" whether he

> likes it or not. A good dictionary may indicate that a particular word (e.g., "ain't") or expression is "unacceptable," but only if the word or expression is so regarded by a great number and variety of speakers of the language. A lexicographer has no right to impose his opinions or the opinions of his social class on all the people. If he is a good language scientist, he will produce a dictionary that describes our language as it is.

When the students had read both passages, the teacher gave them the following questions to answer:

1. Which passage more nearly represents your view? Why?
2. Which passage implies a dictionary ought to resemble a law book?
3. Which passage implies a dictionary ought to resemble a history book?
4. Which passage accepts change in language more easily?
5. Which passage is more concerned with what language is?
6. Which passage is more concerned with what language ought to be?

The discussion that followed was most revealing, and eventually led to a full consideration of the case for and against both prescriptive and descriptive dictionaries. Several students either volunteered or were assigned to read the prefaces of different dictionaries (including *Webster's Third*), and subsequently reported to the rest of the class on some of the striking differences in purpose among dictionaries. In all honesty, it must be reported that the class finally decided to produce "a mostly descriptive but a partly prescriptive" teen-age dictionary. In other words, most of the students perceived that, in the interests of science, their work should be largely descriptive. At the same time, they felt that there would be some value for their readers in their providing clearly labeled opinions and preferences about one matter or another. This being the considered decision of the class, the teacher asked only that the students prepare a carefully written preface to their dictionary, in which they would explain to the reader what kind of dictionary they had made and their reasons for so doing.

When the Preface was completed, the students began the arduous task of collecting items for inclusion in the dictionary. Their original plan for compiling their dictionary was a simple one: Each student would write up proposed entries, each on a 3-x-5 card, and file them in a shoebox in the classroom for subsequent alphabetizing. Two days after they had begun, however, a class session to evaluate their progress revealed problems they had not foreseen. The entries, to begin with, were not uniform in scope or methodology. Some included indications of a word's possible origin; others did not. Some included phonetic spellings, others not. Some indicated the grammatical function or functions of a word, others indicated special circumstances surrounding its usage. Where phonetic spellings and grammatical functions were provided, the systems used varied widely. Students reported problems in spelling their entries (not surprising, since many of the words they proposed had rarely, if ever, appeared in writing). There was the problem of duplication: Many of the students had proposed the same entries. Obviously, the class had to design a more efficient system for collecting, organizing, and reporting their data.

The first problem the students attacked was that of duplication. They created a number of categories of words—words relating to dress, to music, to food, to personal characteristics, and so on—then "signed up" for specialization in a category that particularly interested them, or to which they felt they could contribute most.

The second problem the class dealt with was that of standardizing the form and scope of the entries. Here, the students decided in favor of thoroughness instead of simplicity. ("They were very concerned," reports their teacher, "with producing a 'highly respectable' work.") Each entry would include, in order, the word, its phonetic spelling, a note regarding its origin, its grammatical function or functions, any qualifying comment on its usage, and, finally, its definition.

The class then appointed a number of committees and delegated specific responsibilities to each. The Committee on Phonetic Spelling was asked to research various systems for phonetic spelling, to report its findings to the class, to make recommendations for the Teen-Age Dictionary, to teach the class the system they decided to use, and to serve as the final authority on phonetic spellings in the editing of the work. (This committee, the teacher reports, gave one of the best lessons in phonetic spelling, diacritical marks, and syllabification he's ever seen.) The Committee on Grammatical Functions was assigned similar responsibilities in its field, and the class accepted its majority ruling (there were two strong dissenters) that traditional terminology should be used to indicate grammatical function. The Committee on Origins and Usage had three roles: first, to recommend a form for indicating word origins and to serve as a checkrein on the over-lively imaginations of contributors (who looked on "orig. unk." as a badge of dishonor); second, to research and instruct the class in the correct use of such traditional usage indicators as "obsolete," "slang," "vulgar," "archaic," "colloquial"; third, to devise and teach the class a system for indicating conditions of usage not covered by traditional systems—for example, that the word was used only by girls, or only by boys, or only to disparage. The Committee on Defining investigated and reported to the class on the various methods of defining employed by various dictionaries: defining by synonym, by class and characteristic, by context, by example, and so on. On the recommendation of the Committee, the class decided to provide for each entry (1) a definition by class and characteristic, (2) a connotative definition, (3) two brief contextual definitions, (4) a synonym. Finally, a Committee on Spelling and Alphabetizing was appointed to serve as the final authority on spellings in question, and to assume the task of alphabetizing entries. It was this committee, provoked by one member's plaint that "you always have to know how to spell a word before you can look it up to find its spelling," that proposed listing problem entries according to their likely "misspellings" as well as to their "correct" spellings.

With the new information provided by the committee reports and the more efficient pattern for collecting and organizing data, the students assumed increasing responsibility for independent work on their project. The committees made free use of the bulletin boards in their own and other English classrooms, requesting information on the origins, definitions, and "correct usage" of problem entries. From time to time, the committees requested permission to use part of a class period for discussion of some disputed word. Gradually, the students began to appeal to a wider range of informants for entries. Several students assumed the task of scouring student publications in their own and other schools in the community for words and phrases to include. Others sent letters to friends in other cities. The class requested, and was granted, space in the school newspaper, which the students used to appeal for new information and to verify the data they had already compiled.

About four weeks after they had begun their project, the teacher reports, the students requested his aid in drafting a letter of explanation and an appeal for information, copies of which were sent to the editors of two school newspapers in San Francisco, two in Chicago, two in Houston, two in Miami.

Three weeks later, the students decided in a class meeting that they were ready to assemble their data in final form. Each of the committees exercised its editorial authority in its area of specialization, and the alphabetized 3-x-5 cards were divided among three cooperative typing classes for transfer onto stencils. While the manuscript was being typed and duplicated, the class undertook its final task in the composition of the Teen-Age Dictionary: revising the Preface they had "completed" eight weeks earlier to include sections by the appropriate committees on the phonetic spellings and diacritical marking, methods of defining, origin and usage terminology, and sampling procedures they had employed.

The document these students produced was, in itself, a valuable end. But more valuable by far was the learning generated in the process of producing it. It seems scarcely necessary to catalogue here all that the students learned in the course of the project; indeed, it is doubtful that we could produce an exhaustive catalogue. Obviously, the students learned something about language: phonetic transcription, diacritical marking, syllabification, spelling, word origins, grammatical classifications, usage terminology, defining, alphabetizing, and so forth. Certainly, they learned what dictionaries are, what kinds of information they contain, what points of view they reflect, what problems lexicographers face, what procedures lexicography involves. Most important, these students learned something about the process of inquiry: how to pose relevant questions and devise methods for answering them; to abandon procedures which prove inefficient; to observe, to collect, organize, and verify data; and to communicate the results of inquiry with efficiency. We need hardly argue the superiority of a teaching-learning approach that facilitates the achievement of results such as these over an approach which hopes, at most, "to teach students how to use the dictionary."

Dialect geography. An eleventh-grade class in a Massachusetts high school undertook a highly original research project in dialect geography as an outgrowth of a student's casual question about a novel the class was reading. The novel was *Huckleberry Finn,* and the question was "Did people really talk that way?" Since Twain's use of a written approximation of dialect is one of the remarkable features of his work, the teacher felt the question was a relevant one and worthy of some discussion. It is one of the exciting (and to some teachers, frightening) characteristics of "discovery" teaching that once a question is seriously accepted and the process of inquiry has begun, it is difficult to predict where it will lead and (for the good teacher) even more difficult to cut it off. In this classroom, the original question led, at the end of the period, to another: "Do they still talk that way?"

Because it was an interesting and relevant question, and because it provided unique opportunities for teaching and learning about language, the teacher decided to invite the class to pursue the line of inquiry they had opened. It was an invitation the students eagerly accepted, perhaps because, as Malmstrom and Ashley suggest in *Dialects, U.S.A.,* "all of us are fascinated by comparing our way of saying something with other ways."

The first task the students had to undertake was the reformulation and clarification of the question they wanted to answer: "Do they still talk that way?" To help them begin posing answerable questions, the teacher asked two of her own:

1. Who do you mean by "they"?
2. What do you mean by "that way"?

In answer to the first question, the students decided that "they" meant the people who live in and around the area of Hannibal, Missouri; that is, people who live now where the characters in *Huckleberry Finn* had led their imaginary lives. At their teacher's suggestion, the class decided to select a more limited population for their study (which might otherwise have proved unmanageable); they finally chose to study the dialect spoken by boys of Huck's approximate age in four small towns in a hundred-mile radius around Hannibal.

Answering their teacher's second question, the students found, posed more difficult problems than the first. The students' first response to "What do you mean by 'that way'?" was: "The way Huck talks in the novel." But, as two or three students pointed out, what appears in the novel is writing, not speech. Others added that they could not very efficiently compare Twain's written approximation of speech with the actual sounds of speech recorded on tape. And several students pointed out that they could not possibly compare every utterance of Huck's in the novel with every utterance of their informants in Missouri. Out of these problems grew two specific questions:

1. What system of written symbols could be used to represent and compare the sounds Twain suggested in his approximation of Huck's speech and the sounds of actual speech recorded on tape?
2. What specific characteristics of Huck's speech should the students try to trace in the speech of their informants in Missouri?

To begin answering these questions, the class divided into two groups. The first group assumed the task of researching and reporting to the class alternative notation systems used by dialect geographers to record speech sounds in writing. Their inquiry led them to the school library, and from there to the prefaces of such classic works in dialect geography as *The Linguistic Atlas of the United States and Canada, The Linguistic Atlas of New England,* and *American Dialects,* and to the relevant chapters in such texts as Gleason's *Introduction to Descriptive Linguistics,* and Bloch's *Outline of Linguistic Analysis.* In their report to the class, the members of this research group recommended the use of the simpler IPA system rather than the more exhaustive notation system employed by professional dialect geographers.

While the first group of students researched the problem of notation, the second group devised a plan for selecting the characteristics of Huck's language to be compared with the language of his "real" counterparts. The students decided that a random sample of ten pages of Huck's dialogue would give them an adequate representation of his dialect characteristics, and provide enough items to investigate. From these ten pages, the group composed a list of speech characteristics which they divided into three major categories: vocabulary items, grammatical constructions, and pronunciation. In their final recommendations to the class, the students proposed that their inquiry into the dialect of "Finn-land" focus on twenty-five characteristics of Huck's speech: twelve vocabulary items, five grammatical constructions, and eight typical pronunciation patterns.

The next task facing the class was the translation of Twain's representation of Huck's speech into the symbols of the IPA system. The translation was done in class, with the guidance of two students serving on the "Commission on Speech Notation System." (The teacher notes with some amusement that her students compete to invent the most "scholarly sounding" labels for projects and committees whenever they undertake a sustained inquiry into some aspect of language.)

Having specified the population of their study and organized in useful form the items they wished to investigate, the students were ready to formulate the specific question they wanted to answer and to design procedures for answering it. A class discussion produced the question: "Do the twenty-five speech characteristics of Huckleberry Finn represented in Mark

Twain's novel still appear in the dialect of boys 13–15 years old in the area around Hannibal, Missouri?"

During the next two weeks, the students designed both a questionnaire requesting written answers and a series of questions to be answered orally (the responses of their Missouri informants to be recorded on tape). To insure that their second list of questions would evoke responses likely to include words whose pronunciation and usage they wanted to investigate, the students pretested their "oral-response" questions on thirty-two students in their own school. When they had made the revisions their pretest indicated were necessary, the students felt they were ready to begin collecting their data. Under their teacher's guidance, they drafted a letter describing their project and requesting the cooperation of the teachers and students in four junior-high-school English classes—one in each of four towns near Hannibal. Somewhat surprisingly, each of the first four schools they wrote to responded positively. To each of them, the students sent a set of written questionnaires, a set of oral-response questions, two reels of tape, and a letter to the teacher suggesting procedures to use or to avoid.

While they awaited the return of their questionnaires and tapes, the Massachusetts class set up procedures for organizing and evaluating their raw data. One group of students volunteered for the task of tabulating the responses to the written questionnaire; a second group assumed responsibility for identifying vocabulary items in the recorded responses of their informants; a third group took on the task of listening to the tapes for the grammatical constructions the class had identified as typical of Huck's dialect; and a fourth group volunteered to transcribe in IPA the pronunciations the class had hypothesized would characterize the "Finn-land" dialect.

It is not our intention here to provide you with the information the Massachusetts students gathered, or to reveal the conclusions they reached. Suffice it to say that in the course of their inquiry every student in the class was fully engaged, in one way or another, in behaving as a dialect geographer behaves—which is precisely what their teacher had in mind.

CHAPTER 8

Linguistics and Reading

THERE ARE essentially two kinds of problems involved in learning how to read. The first is sometimes described as the problem of "cracking the code." This means learning to correlate speech (or language) with the written symbols that are used to represent speech. Primary-grade teachers are usually preoccupied with this problem, and when they do their work badly, upper-elementary and even high-school teachers are forced to take an interest in it.

The second problem in learning how to read involves more sophisticated abilities of analyzing, reasoning about, and evaluating language. This problem is quite obviously not *exclusively* a reading problem. As Charles Fries points out in *Linguistics and Reading,* all these abilities can be developed and have been achieved by people who could not read. "They are all matters of the uses of language," Fries writes, "and are not limited to the uses of reading." Nonetheless, there is probably no more urgent need in education than that students learn how to apply such language abilities as thinking, reasoning, judging, and so on to the experiences they have with the written page.

The work of linguists has contributed to an increased understanding of both these problems. In this chapter, we will discuss what these contributions are and what they mean for education.

CRACKING THE CODE (THE BASAL READING SKILLS)

In order to read, one must be able to recognize, more or less automatically, the language signals represented by patterns of graphic shapes. You must know, for example, that the graphic shapes B O Y represent a particular sound pattern of the language. It goes without saying that you are not "reading" if you merely respond to certain graphic shapes by uttering the sounds that they are intended to call forth. This activity is similar to one's "sounding out" a page of a foreign language that one does not know. You *are* reading if you are aware of the correspondence between the sounds you have uttered and their function as some unit of meaning. Just as a baby is not "talking" when it merely imitates a particular sound pattern (for example, "da-dy"), a child is not reading if he is merely "calling words." He is reading only when the graphic shapes on a page direct him toward a meaning response.

None of this, of course, is unfamiliar to teachers of reading. Almost all such teachers can recognize when students have begun to "crack the code," when they are merely "calling words," and when they are unable to understand the problem at all. Linguists, by and large, are no better at identifying these stages than are reading teachers. However, linguists have contributed uniquely to our over-all understanding of what is involved in the process.

Below, we have listed, and elaborated on, four basic ideas taken from the work of linguists, which illuminate and in fact help to define the nature of this early phase of the reading process.

1. *Language is speech.* This is a concept which is often regarded as inane, perhaps because it is so easy to state. And yet, it has far-reaching implications. For example, it reminds us that when a student is first learning to read, he is *not* also first learning language. If he is physiologically normal, the six- or seven-year-old is in full control of the structure of his language (although his vocabulary is obviously limited by his experience). This fact implies that in order to learn how to read, the

student does not first need to be taught the grammatical structure of his language, its sound system, or its intonation patterns. Frequently, teachers of "phonics" plan their work as though the problem were to teach children to speak. As Leonard Bloomfield writes, "Alphabetical writing merely directs the reader to produce certain speech-sounds." A person who cannot produce these sounds cannot read alphabetic writing. But since nearly all six-year-old children can produce these sounds, there is no need for drill in pronunciation.

The idea that language is speech also reminds us that the letters of the alphabet do not "have sounds." Alphabetic writing is a symbolization of speech, a reminding system to the native speaker of something someone has said or could say in the language. The tendency to give young readers the impression that letters have sounds and that words "should be pronounced as they are spelled" often leads to stilted reading and bizarre pronunciations. Students who ask questions like "Do you pronounce the *t* in *often?*" reveal that they are confused about the relation between speech and writing, a confusion that certainly does not facilitate their learning to read efficiently.

2. *Language is structured or patterned.* This concept points to the fact that sentences are not simply individual words strung together in haphazard sequence. As Carl Lefevre observes in *Linguistics and the Teaching of Reading,* a sentence is "a unitary meaning-bearing pattern of grammatical and syntactical functions." In other words, the most significant elements in sentences are not the individual words, but the grammatical structures in which the words are arranged, such as noun and verb clusters. For example, THE FAT CAT is a noun cluster (a structure of modification) which is said with a particular stress pattern, known to any six-year-old. BOYS PLAY is a structure of predication spoken with an equally familiar stress pattern. This fact suggests that a child learning to read should practice reading entire structures rather than individual words. In this way, the child can use normal intonation patterns in reading and avoid word-by-word reading.

Moreover, the emphasis on reading entire structures rather

than individual words makes it much easier to teach the relationship of our punctuation system to speech. Although some punctuation marks are simply a matter of editorial convention, most are attempts to represent pitch and juncture in speech. If students become accustomed to reading with normal intonation patterns, there is every reason to believe that they will master the punctuation system much earlier than they do without such practice.

Finally, since children employ, as a matter of course, rather complex structures when speaking, there is reason to question the wisdom of using, excessively, "baby" sentences as an introduction to the written page.

3. *Our writing system is based on the phonemic, not phonetic, principle.* The letters of the English writing system do not attempt to represent all of the *phones* in English. Rather, they are meant to represent the bundles of sound contrasts that we call *phonemes*. Because teachers frequently assume that the alphabet is phonetic, they teach sounds as isolated units. For example, they will show children the letter *t,* and try to make them react by uttering a corresponding sound. English-speaking people are not accustomed to making that kind of noise. As Bloomfield writes: "The sound (t) does not occur alone in English utterances; neither does the sound (t) followed by an obscure vowel sound. If we insist on making the child perform unaccustomed feats with his vocal organs, we are bound to confuse his response to the printed signs. In any language, most phonemes do not occur by themselves, in isolated utterance, and even most of the successions of phonemes which one could theoretically devise, are never so uttered." In other words, one simply cannot pronounce the phoneme *t*. One can pronounce an allophone of it, as in the word *top,* or in the word *pot,* or as in the word *stop*. Each of these allophones is pronounced differently. The pronunciation used is determined by the environment in which the allophone is located. This suggests that in helping to familiarize students with the sounds that letters represent, teachers should always provide a realistic, utterable context.

Moreover, the assumption that the alphabet is based on a

phonetic principle rather than a phonemic one often leads to an unrealistic insistence on a single standard of pronunciation. For example, the pronunciations of the word *house* vary greatly in American dialects. It is obvious that the letters *ou* are intended to represent all the allophones of the vowel in question, and are not intended to represent a specific single sound. The letters, in other words, remind us of a particular phoneme, not a particular phone, and a phoneme, you will recall, is a kind of abstraction that includes a variety or range of specific sounds. If teachers wish to change the pronunciations of their students, they must not do so by using the writing system as a justification. In fact, our phonemically based writing system encourages readers to employ their particular dialects.

4. *Our writing system is patterned.* We have been careful to say that our writing system is based on the "phonemic principle." Strictly speaking, it is not phonemic. An authentic phonemic alphabet would have one symbol for each of the separate phonemes of our language; that is, there would be a 1 to 1 correspondence between a bundle of sounds and a graphic shape. Of course, the inconsistencies in our writing system have been widely parodied, and are, in any case, well known. Usually, one points to the variety of sounds represented by the letter-combination *ough,* or to the variety of ways in which we graphically represent the sound [i]; for example, *we, seize, key, meat, machine, meet, people.* Nevertheless, it can be demonstrated that there is considerable regularity in our writing system. Probably the most significantly consistent arrangement of spelling patterns are those for one-syllable words representing consonant-vowel-consonant, such as *bat, fat, hat, gat, mat, rat, sat* or *cot, dot, got, hot, lot.* There are consistent variations of this pattern, as in the case of *bat, bag, bad, ban* or *hat, hag, had, ham.*

A second set of consistent spelling patterns are those that use the final letter *e* to differentiate between *hat* and *hate;* for example, *dam* and *dame, lam* and *lame, rob* and *robe, cop* and *cope.* Generally speaking, linguists believe that the teaching of reading can be done more efficiently if teachers and writers of reading texts were fully aware of these regularities and put them at the heart of instruction. Of course, most reading teachers intuitively work in this direction, but the assumption is that their work would be more successful if it were based on a systematic understanding and presentation of spelling regularity.

The question must now be asked: How successful have linguists been in utilizing these concepts in textbooks and reading programs? The answer is, We don't know yet. As early as 1937, Leonard Bloomfield concerned himself with these problems. However, his *Let's Read* series has not been used widely enough to warrant a clear verdict, although those who have used it believe it to be a vast improvement over traditional texts. More recently, Charles Fries, Henry Lee Smith, Jr., and Paul Roberts have produced materials based on the concepts we have described, but it is too soon to make a judgment about them. We find ourselves in general agreement with Albert Marckwardt, who has observed that "linguistically oriented textbooks for the teaching of reading are fairly recent in their development and cannot be said to have much more than initial trials." The same may be said for such programs as the Initial Teaching Alphabet and Unifon, both of which are attempts to substitute a more uniform symbol system for our traditional orthography. Both systems are, of course, based on the phonemic principle, and are intended to reduce the amount of frustration and failure that children experience when they first encounter the written page. The assumption is that if we build the confidence of young readers in their ability to "crack a writing code," they can more easily learn (say, by the second or third grade) how to crack the conventional code.

THE THINKING PROBLEM IN READING

This phase of the reading process involves all of the abilities suggested by such words as *thinking, reasoning, imagining, judging;* in other words, those abilities we particularly stressed in the chapter on semantics. Here, we are not dealing with phonemes, allophones, intonation patterns, or punctuation. This phase of the reading process assumes that the reader has solved most of the problems normally associated with learning to correlate written symbols with speech.

In fact, it is worth observing at this point that it is unfortunate the word *linguistics* so frequently calls to mind such physical mechanisms of language as, say, its phonemic or allophonic structure. Dr. Emmett Betts has written: "In some schools, teachers limit their discussions of 'linguistics and reading' to phonemics. This limited view tends to ignore the possible contributions of linguistics to the thinking facet of reading instruction. In fact, linguistics embraces not only the phonemic structure of language, but the grammatical structure as well." It is encouraging to know that we are beginning to recognize that what we call *thinking* is somehow related to what we call grammatical structure, and certainly Dr. Betts is right in saying that linguists have something of value to offer reading teachers in this regard. But we would insist upon going even further than Dr. Betts: If one is interested in what he calls "the thinking facet of reading instruction," one should challenge linguistics to provide not just a description of the operations of language but also a description of the operations of language users.

Wendell Johnson once remarked that the most significant development in psychology in our time is the discovery by psychologists that human beings *talk*. Similarly, some linguists are beginning to discover that the subject they study, language, is produced by human beings, to serve human purposes. They are discovering, in short, that the proper study of language is the study of man, and that there is no good reason why a linguist cannot or should not study man, the language user. Many linguists have avoided doing so because such inquiries would inevitably lead them into the processes of human psychology. Theirs is an understandable timidity, for it is easier to describe phonemes than phobias. But let us face the fact: The study of that human process we call language *is* fundamentally a study in human psychology, and those who are interested in teaching reading will continue to blench and stammer a little when they talk about "the thinking facet" of reading until they fix their gaze on the language user as well as his language.

I. A. Richards once commented on the superficiality of some interpretations of poetry by saying, "We pay attention to externals when we do not know what else to do with a poem." If we may paraphrase Richards' remark, in the study of reading, too often we pay attention to externals because we don't know what else to study.

We come, then, to some of the more relevant and fruitful lines of inquiry into the reading process that linguistics allows us to follow. In a recent article entitled "How Do Students Read a Short Story?" Ruth Strang and Charlotte Rogers pose the question, What kind of thinking or reasoning goes on in a student's mind when he reads a short story, a popular article, a textbook in science or history? From our point of view, there is no more important type of question to ask about the reading process than that. Variations of the question are: What do people *do* when they read? Why do they give meanings to, or withhold meanings from, words they perceive on paper? What are the characteristics of the behavior we call "misreading?"

These questions, of course, contain certain assumptions that need to be articulated in some detail. The major assumption underlying these questions is, as semanticists would say, that words appearing on a page do not *by themselves* have meaning. Meaning is supplied to words by a human nervous system. If no human nervous system makes an attempt to give meaning to black marks appearing on white paper, then there is no meaning to be talked about.

Some of you might be thinking at this point that we are saying, If there were no people on earth, but there did exist all the books that have been printed, then those books would contain no meaning. And that is precisely what we are saying. Meaning is what *results* from the transaction between language and language user. If neither one is present, no meaning can exist. If you believe that the play *Hamlet* somehow *means* something whether anyone looks at it or not, we can only account for that illusion by saying that it is based on the fact that you (and others) have already assigned meaning to *Hamlet;* and, further, that it is based on the inference that those who have not yet assigned meaning to it would be capable of doing so if they were confronted with the text.

Although what we are saying probably seems obvious to you, we can assure you that the notion that words have inherent meanings, *real* meanings—that words *possess* meanings quite apart from what human beings do with words—is very widespread. Not long ago, we heard an English teacher caution her students against using the word *dilapidated* unless they meant by it "an old stone wall." That, she said, was its *real* meaning.

Many teachers of reading, and therefore the students they instruct, believe that the process of reading involves discovering the "real" meaning of a passage. They seem to believe that the reader is neither expected nor entitled to play a role in creating the meaning of a passage. Their basic metaphor of the reading process is that the material supplied by an author is something like a completed structure whose height, width, depth, and texture can be described if only the reader looks at it hard enough and employs appropriate instruments.

Probably a more realistic metaphor is that the reading material supplied by the author is like a *blueprint* for a building, and each reader constructs from the blueprint a structure that is, in its detail, uniquely his own.

Perhaps some brief illustrations will serve to clarify this point. A few years ago, an interview with Supreme Court Justice Hugo Black was published in the New York University *Law Review*. Justice Black talked about the phrase in the Constitution that states that Congress shall make *no law* abridging the freedom of speech. According to Justice Black, the phrase is absolutely clear. It means NO LAW. Nothing, zero, cipher. He gave notice, therefore, that he, at least, was prepared to declare unconstitutional all slander and libel laws. But quite obviously, Justice Black's reading of this phrase from the Constitution differs strikingly from the readings made by other Supreme Court Justices. It is not likely that we will ever have five Justices who will build the same kind of structure from that phrase that Justice Black did.

To take one more example from the experience of the Supreme Court (whose reading processes are always of great public interest), let us look at the interesting reading of the phrase "separate but equal." In 1896, a majority of the Supreme Court Justices gave to that phrase a meaning that rendered it consistent with our understanding of equality under the law. In 1954, however, a new group of readers unanimously agreed to assign to the phrase "separate but equal" quite a different meaning. The words "separate" and "equal," they said, are in this context *antonyms;* therefore, the phrase is self-contradictory. In their own words, "Separate but equal is inherently unequal." It is, in short, unproductive to ask, "But what does 'separate but equal' *really* mean?" Rather, one must ask, "What will these people make it mean? And for what reasons? And in what circumstances?"

If meaning did inhere in words and not in people, then all Supreme Court decisions would be 9 to 0, and, once made, would stand for all time. Quite obviously, this is not the case. In terms of our metaphor, each Supreme Court Justice takes the Constitution as a blueprint, and each builds from it a structure of meaning which is, in its detail, unique.

All teachers of reading know that some readers, in the face of a particular blueprint, will not be able to build a finished structure. They know, too, that some readers confronted with a blueprint will construct a building that cannot stand. We come then to the question, What kinds of behavior are exhibited when readers are in the process of doing what we call "misreading"?

The best inquiry into this basic question was conducted many years ago by I. A. Richards. It is not easy to find a suitable professional label for Richards, but in his explorations of how people read—and therefore of how people misread—he employed the characteristic way of behaving used by linguists. That is, he approached his subject with an open mind; he phrased answerable questions; he collected empirical data; he classified his data into what seemed to him meaningful patterns; he analyzed his data; then he drew his conclusions.

Richards' studies were conducted at Cambridge, Harvard, and Radcliffe, and his subjects were students at those great universities. Quite simply, what Richards did was as follows: He presented his students with material to read. He invited them to write unstructured reactions to this material; that is, he did not organize their responses for them by asking them specific questions about the material. He carefully catalogued their responses, always focusing on the question, "What were these readers trying to do?" As a result of his inquiry, Richards identified at least ten patterns of misreading among his subjects. It goes without saying that each of his categories of misreading describes a psychological process of the reader; that is, his categories describe types of behavior exhibited by readers as they transact with language.

Perhaps two examples will clarify the nature of Richards' categories of misreading. One of his categories is what he calls the "doctrinal adhesion." By this he means that there are some readers with such strong political, moral, theological, or social commitments that they are prevented from giving to a passage meanings that would conflict with their own ideologies. In other words, the author's blueprint has perhaps called for the construction of some kind of synagogue, but the reader insists on building a cathedral. To shift the metaphor, the reader's political, theological, moral, or social biases act as a screen between him and the material he is reading, preventing him from seeing reasonable possibilities of meaning. In other words, what is happening is that the reader rejects the invitation to enter into the reality of another man because that reality is, from his (the reader's) point of view, objectionable.

Some other psychological processes that Richards perceived are what he calls "technical presuppositions" and "general critical preconceptions." To use our metaphor again, what seems to be happening here is that the reader rejects the blueprint that the writer has provided, because he feels that there can be no building constructed from such a blueprint. Such a reader often judges the whole by the detail, instead of the other way about. For example, he may have a notion that a paragraph must always begin with what he calls a "topic sentence," and if it does not, the paragraph will seem unclear to him. In the case of poetry, he may believe that all poems should have a definite rhyme scheme, and he will not participate in building a meaningful poem if it does not. He will say, "This is prose" or "This is sloppy." He may believe that "dilapidated" must always be used to mean "an old stone wall," and he will have no truck with any writing whose context suggests some other meaning.

In this connection, it is appropriate to remark that a good deal of the instruction given to students in their English classes contributes to their becoming poor readers in Richards' terms. The student, for example, who effectively learns the grammatical "rule" that a pronoun must always have a clear antecedent might have considerable difficulty with many of Robert Frost's poems. Similarly, the student who brings to the reading experience the notion that metaphors should never be mixed will predictably have difficulty with "taking arms against a sea of troubles." We have even found an eleventh-grade student, no doubt extraordinarily attentive in his vocabulary lessons, who found the following line from the Gettysburg Address "defective": "The brave men, living and dead, who struggled here, have consecrated it far above our poor power to add or detract." His comment was that if Lincoln was going to be quantitative, he should have said "add or *subtract*." Mercifully, the student did not say that "of the people, by the people, and for the people" was either repetitious or superfluous.

The best description we know of the way in which critical preconceptions and technical presuppositions operate to cause misreadings was provided by W. Somerset Maugham in *The Summing Up*. The description is also a perfect illustration of how language teaching can foster reading blocks:

> I have never had more than two English lessons in my life, for though I wrote essays at school, I do not remember that I ever received any instruction on how to put sentences together. The two lessons I have had were given me so late in life that I am afraid I cannot hope greatly to profit by them. The first was only a few years ago. I was spending some weeks in London and had engaged as temporary secretary a young woman. She was shy, rather pretty, and absorbed in a love affair with a married man. I had written a book called *Cakes and Ale* and, the typescript arriving one Saturday morning, I asked her if she would be good enough to take it home and correct it over the week-end. I meant her only to make a note of mistakes

> in spelling that the typist might have made and point out errors occasioned by a handwriting that is not always easy to decipher. But she was a conscientious young person and she took me more literally than I intended. When she brought back the transcript on Monday morning it was accompanied by four foolscap sheets of corrections. I must confess that at the first glance I was a trifle vexed; but then I thought that it would be silly of me not to profit, if I could, by the trouble she had taken and so sat me down to examine them. I suppose the young woman had taken a course at a secretarial college and she had gone through my novel in the same methodical way as her masters had gone through her essays. The remarks that filled the four neat pages of foolscap were incisive and severe. I could not but surmise that the professor of English at the secretarial college did not mince matters. He took a marked line, there could be no doubt about that; and he did not allow that there might be two opinions about anything. His apt pupil would have nothing to do with a preposition at the end of a sentence. A mark of exclamation betokened her disapproval of a colloquial phrase. She had a feeling that you must not use the same word twice on a page and she was ready every time with a synonym to put in its place. If I had indulged myself in the luxury of a sentence of ten lines, she wrote: "Clarify this. Better break it up into two or more periods." When I had availed myself of the pleasant pause that is indicated by a semicolon, she noted: "A full stop"; and if I had ventured upon a colon she remarked stingingly: "Obsolete." But the harshest stroke of all was her comment on what I thought was rather a good joke: "Are you sure of your facts?" Taking it all in all I am bound to conclude that the professor at her college would not have given me very high marks.

The type of inquiry conducted by Richards has been pursued, with important modifications, by several workers, although, in our opinion, not nearly as many as the inquiry warrants. In general, they have tried to study the nature of the responses of junior- and senior-high-school students rather than university students (as did Richards). But, like Richards, they have used the responses of students as their empirical data, and have tried to identify specific patterns of behavior that cause difficulty for students in reading. Among those who have engaged in this kind of inquiry are James Squire (*The Responses of Adolescents While Reading Four Short Stories*); Mildred Letton (*Individual Differences in Interpretive Responses in Reading Poetry at the Ninth Grade Level*); and Charlotte Dee Rogers (*Individual Differences in Interpretive Responses to Reading the Short Story at the Eleventh Grade Level*). All of them are indebted to Richards and to Professor Louise Rosenblatt, whose book *Literature as Exploration* (1939) first articulated for the profession at large the educational implications of this approach to the reading process.

One of the great advantages of such a research program is that almost any teacher of reading—English teacher or otherwise—can participate in the process of collecting a body of material for analysis and, to some extent, in helping to analyze it. If, for example, we could assemble a large body of responses from students in various parts of the country, we might discover that, to a certain extent, a particular reading problem is unique to a geographical region, a socio-economic class, an ethnic or religious group. We suspect, in fact, that this would be the case. With the kind permission of Raymond Arlo, we can illustrate this point by reproducing below some of the responses of two different groups to which he gave the following passage, requesting their individual reactions:

> "Lawd, we ain't what we wanna be; we ain't what we oughta be; we sho' nuff ain't what we lak ta be; but thank the Lawd, we ain't what we was."

The first group consisted of English teachers in a suburban community near New York City. Here are some of their comments:

1. Grammatically this is terrible.
2. This is an unnatural way of speaking English.
3. I think it is good English. It can be used as a sample of a dialect and a beautiful one, too. We should teach this

in class, along with Shakespeare and Chaucer and perhaps E. E. Cummings.

4. I feel sorry for him because he wants to better himself but he can't. I *do not* mark him as stupid. I mark him as being uneducated because of his "way of speaking."

5. This sentence is clear in meaning. However, it is socially incorrect in its profuse use of unacceptable (to our society) words such as "ain't."

6. There is nothing wrong with writing or speaking in this form of English as long as we all agreed to speak the same way, but for the splinter groups to have their own language derived from English is not really defensible on the grounds it can be understood.

7. My reaction is a sympathetic smile; I would like to help, but, you see, I can't right now. . . . Perhaps it is because I feel the speaker just has not helped himself along enough (to speak "good English") to warrant help from me.

8. The word "Lawd" has no connection with the rest of the sentence. . . . I disliked the above structure because of the great number of its mistakes and my main object being the learning of English, I would rather not come across many sentences of that kind.

The second group of readers consisted of ninth-grade students in a junior high school in New York City. Here are some of *their* comments:

1. I like this statement, and it only goes to prove that life is a precious thing.

2. I like it. It says just what the speaker is trying to get across to God.

3. I'll bet God will listen to this man better than to a lot of others.

4. I think that this is being said by a Negro preacher who is telling God that although things haven't been so good, there's still plenty to be thankful for.

There were, of course, among the second group, many responses similar to those that came from the first group. It doesn't take too long before students develop the same reading blocks as their teacher. Nevertheless, when the responses are compared, several striking differences are clear. The readers in Group I are unanimous in their preoccupation with the grammar of the statement. Not one of them comments on the fact that this brief passage is apparently a prayer—in fact, one of these readers, not knowing how to deal with an ungrammatical prayer, says explicitly, "The word 'Lawd' has no connection with the rest of the sentence." Even the one teacher who liked the passage stresses that it is written in a "dialect." The most interesting aspect of the reading behavior of Group I is that *all* the respondents refused to give to the passage any *meaning,* in a referential sense.

The readers in Group II struggle more directly with the problem of giving meaning to the passage, and all of them seem to recognize that it is a philosophic statement of some kind.

The responses to this passage, in short, suggest that the students read it more intelligently than the teachers. Obviously, this is not always the case (although it is by no means rare). Below, for example, are two responses to two different poems. Both were provided by seniors in high school (and we are indebted once again to Mr. Arlo for permission to use them here). We think the responses do not warrant comment from us, except to say that they reveal the magnitude of the problem of teaching reading.

The first response is to the poem "The Golf Links" by Sarah N. Cleghorn:

THE GOLF LINKS

The golf links lie so near the mill
  That almost every day
The laboring children can look out
  And see the men at play.

Here is the student's response:

> I see a mill like in Holland, windmill and little kids about 9 years old working around it. Near the mill you see a golf course where men are playing. From this picture I get the idea that in starting life you work hard and conscientiously later on in life you have established your funds and staples so that there will be more time to enjoy life and what it has to offer. The children are now at the start of life, building their future. They are able to see what hard work and success will bring as they see the men playing.

The next response is to the poem "Richard Cory," by Edwin Arlington Robinson:

> Richard Cory was a very rich man. I see him as the owner of almost everything in a town where everyone is working for him. He is very cordial to everyone he meets, but the people working for him dislike his greedy inner self. He had money and power but he was lonely so one night he went home and killed himself. Richard Cory could represent communism, the people are those living under this dictator, and the shooting of Cory the downfall of communism. When downtown, or in the eyes of prospective communist nations, Richard Cory has a golden heart, but the people living and working for him see the true Richard Cory and hate what he stands for, and therefore rebel and overthrow the communist government.

The reading difficulties of these students were not developed overnight. They probably had their beginnings when the students were in the third or fourth grades. Below are two illustrations of reading problems in the making.

On the very first page of a recently published third-grade textbook, the students are introduced to a poem by this "motivating" statement: "The following poem is about lambs that are born in the wintertime. The only world they know is cold and filled with snow. They have no idea of the spring that is to come."

One might well ask precisely what this statement motivates the students to do. It is intended, obviously, to stimulate them to read the poem. But why should they? They've already been told what it's all about. From our point of view, "motivating" statements of this kind "motivate" long-range attitudes toward poetry, and ways of behaving when confronted with it, that are far from productive. What the student is learning here, at least in part, is to rely on the pronouncements of an authority for clues to "the meaning" of a poem and directions for responding to it. The "motivating" statement preceding a poem (or any other literary work) often, as in this instance, renders fruitless and irrelevant the key question, "What do you think this poem is about?" The student has no *need* to think, when the authoritative voice of the text's author has already structured his perception of the poem. Such statements insure that the reading process is short-circuited. The student learns not to read a poem, not to enjoy making it his own by ascribing his own meanings to it, but to read someone else's meanings.

Following the "motivating" paragraph we have quoted is a paragraph of directions to the student that includes this line: "Notice the details, so that you will be able to answer questions about them." Need we point out the probable effect of such a direction on the attitude of the student toward the reading of poetry?

In the same textbook there appears the following poem by Eleanor Farjeon:

JENNY WHITE AND JOHNNY BLACK

Jenny White and Johnny Black
Went out for a walk.
Jenny found wild strawberries,
And John a lump of chalk.

Jenny White and Johnny Black
Clambered up a hill.
Jenny heard a willow-wren
And John a workman's drill.

Jenny White and Johnny Black
Wandered by the dike.

Jenny smelt the meadow-sweet,
And John a motor-bike.

Jenny White and Johnny Black
Turned into a lane.
Jenny saw the moon by day,
And Johnny saw a train.

Jenny White and Johnny Black
Walked into a storm.
Each felt for the other's hand
And found it nice and warm.

In his commentary to the teacher, the author of the textbook begins: "The names in this poem have no special significance. The poet might just as well have chosen the names 'Jenny Jones' and 'Johnny Smith.'"

But the poet did *not* choose "Jenny Jones" and "Johnny Smith"; she chose—and one must assume that the word choices of poets are deliberate and significant—"Jenny White" and "Johnny Black." Indeed, the names seem to be of such significance that the poet chose to title her poem with them. Of course, if we follow our author's line of reasoning, she might just as well have titled the poem "Differences" or "Romanticism and Realism." Once we have decided to take this tack, there is almost no reading of the poem we could not eliminate on the grounds that x, y, and z words are not significant. As a matter of fact, the author of the textbook comes close to doing precisely that when he adds the comment that the fact that Jenny is a girl and Johnny is a boy is not especially significant either.

From our point of view, there is sufficient internal evidence in the poem (the last stanza, for example) to support the possible reading that "Jenny is white and Johnny is black"—but this is not the key issue here. What is of critical importance is the effect on the student's reading behavior of being told, in an entirely arbitrary manner, that such and so meanings must be excluded because such and so words are not significant. As we indicated earlier, the process of learning to read is the process of learning to ascribe or withhold meanings, of learning to determine what is and is not significant and why. How is the student to learn to read if his teacher and his textbook do not permit him to engage freely in these processes?

To point out just one more likely source of future reading problems, we need to comment on still another piece of advice in the teacher's material accompanying "Jenny White and Johnny Black." Referring to a composition assignment based on the poem, the author writes:

> It is important that the children write about one or the other of the people and not both. Otherwise they will tend simply to repeat the content of the poem. The assignment gives the child a chance to write about *the real meaning of the poem* [italics ours]. Since the point will already have been discussed, some children, at least, should succeed.

While we find this paragraph full of questionable assumptions (e.g., that the child can write about *any* meaning of the poem without referring to the relationship between two people), what seems to us most dangerous is the phrase we have italicized. As we indicated earlier, one of the major stumbling blocks to intelligent reading is the belief that a poem has one *real* meaning, which the reader must "dig out." Needless to say, the teacher or text who sets the student out on the fruitless search for "real" meanings is not helping him to read.

Research into the reading problems of students is by no means confined to the analysis of responses to what is called "literature." To illustrate: the story is told of a pregnant woman who visited her obstetrician in a state of terror. She told him that she had four children at home, and she had read that every fifth child born in the world is Chinese. This woman has a reading problem that is not as far-fetched as you might think. One teacher gave the following passage to a group of fifth-graders. It is taken from Dr. Benjamin Spock's book, *Baby and Child Care*. The passage reads as follows:

> Usually the first two teeth are the central incisors. After a few months come the four upper incisors. The average baby has these six teeth, four above and two below, when he is a year old.

When asked to respond to the relatively unstructured question, "What does this passage mean to you?" not more than one out of three readers gave any indication of an awareness that Dr. Spock is apparently talking about a hypothetical baby. In other words, there was a general failure to distinguish between statistical reality and literal reality. One supposes this kind of misreading can be included in a category called, perhaps, Confusion of Levels of Abstraction.

We said before that this kind of research has a great advantage in that any teacher of reading can participate in it. But this kind of research is also a method of teaching reading. Students can learn how to read better by studying *what they do* when they try to read. In other words, each student can become a research worker into his own reading problems. The role of the reader is to give reasonable meanings to what is written. If the reader is allowed to respond freely to writing, he may then use his own response as the focus of inquiry. The reader, in this way, becomes his own linguist. He must ask himself, "What are my reasons for assigning these meanings to this passage? How can I justify or document the reasonableness of these meanings in this context? To what extent have I given attention to all the elements in the author's blueprint? Which elements have I emphasized? Which elements have I slighted? What justification can I offer for doing so?" Moreover, there is no reason why a group of students, with the guidance of their teacher, could not engage in inquiries into the ways in which meanings are made.

What we are saying is that students can try to find out what people do in their efforts to create meaning from the written word. They can begin their investigation by taking their own responses to the written page as their data, and they can infer from these responses *how* they do their reading: what attitudes help or hinder them; what beliefs facilitate or block the creation of reasonable meanings; what information adds to or detracts from their ability to apply appropriately the meanings that written materials suggest.

CHAPTER 9

Beyond Linguistics

VARIOUS WAYS of looking at language have emerged from linguistics and seem to extend beyond it. Two prominent and current extensions of linguistics are, first, *metalinguistics* and, second, *psycholinguistics*. The difference between these two perspectives and, for that matter, between these two and semantics, may be difficult to discern. They become clearer as the definitions become more operational.

Metalinguistics, as the term is now used, refers to the study of mutual relationships between language behavior and other modes of human behavior. Metalinguistics goes beyond microlinguistics. Microlinguistics can be regarded as synonymous with descriptive linguistics, the study of differential meanings in language forms. In microlinguistics the focus is on the component parts of sentences, or smaller units of language; that is, its focus is on clauses, phrases, words, morphemes, phonemes, and so on—the formal units of language. Metalinguistics extends to include an examination of a total universe of discourse and the relations between this and the rest of a culture. Because an older definition of metalinguistics, in philosophy, referred to it as a theory of language about language, another term, *exolinguistics,* has been advocated. In this context, as a concession to common currency, only the term metalinguistics will be used.

Benjamin Lee Whorf produced the main body of work from

which *metalinguistics* developed (and is developing). While the details of Whorf's involvement in linguistics are fascinating, they are beyond the scope of our modest mention. (Anyone interested in more detail must see *Language, Thought, and Reality,* edited by John B. Carroll.) Suffice it to say that he engaged in his examination, largely of American Indian languages, under the guidance of Edward Sapir at Yale, and learned to use the tools of linguistic analysis, not "for their own sake," but specifically for the purpose of developing an understanding of the mutual (and largely "invisible") transactions among language, thought, and reality. Whorf's study led him to formulate the hypothesis which today bears his name and from which metalinguistics is developing.

In its simplest terms, Whorf's hypothesis states that the structure of the language one uses "shapes" not only how one thinks, but what one can think about. In this view, language is not merely a vehicle for expressing thought, it is also the driver. Or, to shift the metaphor, language is related to thought in somewhat the way in which a musical instrument is related to the sounds it makes. No matter how various are the tunes one can play, the instrument one uses limits what can be played. You cannot make the sound of a rolling drum on a clarinet. You cannot make the sound of a trumpet on a violin. Thus, the "tune" that you call "thinking" is the product of the structure of your particular language instrument.

Some academic linguists do not view this proposition with sympathy, usually describing it as metaphysical. Nonetheless, Whorf's hypothesis is not new. Observations on the mutual relationships between language and thought have been made by many thinkers of distinction. Plato, for example, has Socrates say, "When the mind is thinking, it is talking to itself." Hobbes saw language and thought as inseparable, and recognized that without language knowlege could not exist. Locke reaffirmed Hobbes's insight: "Knowledge . . . has had greater connexion with words than is commonly suspected. . . ." Leibniz (who otherwise disagreed with him) was in complete accord with Locke on this point. The German philologist Max Müller maintained "that thought cannot exist without signs, and that our most important signs are words." A very Whorfian-type remark.

In the twentieth century, many other contributors to metalinguistics (including most of those mentioned earlier in the section on Semantics) appear. Their names are associated with a diversity of disciplines other than linguistics, with psychology and sociology, not surprisingly, quite prominent. In 1918, for example, J. Ward said, in *Psychological Principles,* that while thought may originate without language, it is with (or through) the use of symbols that thinking grows in a geometric pattern. As a simple matter of fact, I.Q. tests (except those specifically designed to measure nonverbal intelligence) are based on this thesis.

In order to get a sense of what is meant by the suggestion that thought occurs "in" a language, you might try to work out a simple arithmetic problem—in multiplication, for example—first using Arabic and then Roman numerals. The basic principle of magnitude in Roman numerals is a function of repetition. The "simple" symbol zero permits a kind of thinking at a rate that is inconceivable to someone who has only Roman numerals in his repertoire. The fact that different kinds of mathematics (i.e., different methods of thinking) permit different intellectual operations to occur, and for that matter permit only certain kinds of "quantities" to be perceived in the first place, helps to lend credence to the Whorfian hypothesis.

Whorf's study of American Indian languages permitted him to detect a range of linguistic differences that would not have been possible had he confined his studies to European languages. To quote Whorf:

> . . . we all, unknowingly, project the linguistic relationships of a particular language upon the universe, and *see* them there. . . . We say "see that wave"—the same pattern as "see that house." But without the projection of language no one ever saw a single wave. We see a surface in ever-changing undulating motions. Some languages cannot say "a wave"; they are closer to reality in this respect. Hopi

say *walatata,* "plural waving occurs," and can call attention to one place in the waving just as we can. But since actually a wave cannot exist by itself, the form which corresponds to our singular, *wala,* is not the equivalent of English "a wave," but means "a slosh occurs," as when a vessel of liquid is suddenly jarred.

English pattern treats "I hold it" exactly like "I strike it," "I tear it," and myriads of other propositions that refer to actions effecting changes in matter. Yet "hold" in plain fact is no action, but a state of relative positions. But we think of it, even see it, as an action, because language sets up the proposition in the same way as it sets up a much more common class of propositions dealing with movements and changes. We ascribe action to what we call "hold" because the formula, substantive + verb = actor + his action, is fundamental in our sentences. Thus we are compelled in many cases to read into nature fictitious acting-entities simply because our sentence patterns require our verbs, when not imperative, to have substantives before them. We are obliged to say "it flashed" or "a light flashed," setting up an actor, *it,* or *a light,* to perform what we call an action, *flash.* But the flashing and the light are the same; there is no thing which does something, and no doing. Hopi says only *rehpi.* Hopi can have verbs without subjects, and this gives to that language power as a logical system for understanding certain aspects of the cosmos. Scientific language, being founded on western Indo-European and not on Hopi, does as we do, sees sometimes actions and forces where there may be only states. For do you not conceive it possible that scientists as well as ladies with cats all unknowingly project the linguistic patterns of a particular type of language upon the universe, and *see* them there, rendered visible on the very face of nature? A change in language can transform our appreciation of the cosmos.—"Language, Mind, and Reality," *ETC.*, LX, No. 3 (Spring, 1952; special issue on "Metalinguistics").

Whorf's conclusion to this paragraph, originally published in 1942, is particularly timely. Philipp Frank, for example, in his book *Einstein, His Life and Times* specifically refers to the scientific revolution, in the sense conveyed best, perhaps, by his statement: "Einstein's *relativity of time* is a reform in *semantics,* not in metaphysics."

Support for a Whorfian metalinguistic view comes from other directions as well. Students of Oriental philosophy and languages have commented on the striking differences between Western and Eastern thought, attributable in large measure to the differences in the "instruments" (languages) with which Easterners and Westerners do their thinking. In *The Way of Zen,* Alan Watts provides a "metalinguistic" explanation of such differences:

> The reason why Taoism and Zen present, at first sight, such a puzzle to the Western mind is that we have taken a restricted view of human knowledge. For us, almost all knowledge is what a Taoist would call *conventional* knowledge, because we do not feel that we really know anything unless we can represent it to ourselves in words, or in some other system of conventional signs such as the notations of mathematics and music. Such knowledge is called conventional because it is a matter of social agreement as to the codes of communication. Just as people speaking the same language have tacit agreements as to what words shall stand for what things, so the members of every society and every culture are united by bonds of communication resting upon all kinds of agreement as to the classification and valuation of actions and things.
>
> Thus the task of education is to make children fit to live in a society by persuading them to learn and accept its codes—the rules and conventions of communication whereby the society holds itself together. There is first the spoken language. The child is taught to accept "tree" and and not "boojum" as the agreed sign for *that* (pointing to the object). We have no difficulty in understanding that the word "tree" is a matter of convention. What is much less obvious is that convention also governs the delineation of the thing to which the word is assigned. For the child has to be taught not only what words are to stand for what

things, but also the way in which his culture has tacitly agreed to divide things from each other, to mark out the boundaries within our daily experience. Thus, scientific convention decides whether an eel shall be a fish or a snake, and grammatical convention determines what experiences shall be called objects and what shall be called events or actions. How arbitrary such conventions may be can be seen from the question, "What happens to my fist (noun-object) when I open my hand?" The object miraculously vanishes because an action was disguised by a part of speech usually assigned to a thing! In English the differences between things and actions are clearly, if not always logically, distinguished, but a great number of Chinese words do duty for both nouns and verbs—so that one who thinks in Chinese has little difficulty in seeing that objects are also events, that our world is a collection of processes rather than entities.

At the present moment, metalinguistics seems to be just beyond the linguist's terrain, doubtless because it does not lend itself to the usual methods of inquiry. This fact, in itself, is a kind of metalinguistic problem, since the ground rules of respectable scientific inquiry are a product, as a Taoist would say, of the conventional modes of communication. Nonetheless, it must be noted that at least one linguist, Anatol Rapoport, has designed a study that attempts to test the validity of certain assumptions of metalinguistics. As of this writing, we do not have knowlege of any findings.

The second extension of linguistics, and one which may come to dominate the study of language, if present developments are any indication, is what is most commonly called *psycholinguistics.* This form of linguistic investigation concentrates on verbal behavior, and seems to go by a number of names: psychology of speech, psychology of language, linguistic psychology, and even psychology of communication. Once again, this "field" is not very neat, its contributors coming from virtually every subcategory of psychology. Just as linguists have been reluctant to connect with psychology, psychologists have been slow to undertake a study of language as behavior. The reasons for this are, of course, complex, but we might venture an oversimplified explanation. Psychology up until recently has been shaped by the largely mechanistic metaphors of early-twentieth-century behaviorism; that is, all behavior was viewed almost exclusively as relatively mechanical responses to stimuli. We have all seen the key symbol of this approach: S-R. It was not until recently that it was suggested that an *O* be inserted between the *S* and *R* in recognition of the fact that it was an organism that was being stimulated and that was doing the responding. This line of thinking led to the development of phenomenological psychology and what is now called perceptual psychology, both of which are complementary to transactional psychology.

These approaches to psychology focus on the point of view, or perception, of the individual as a key element in determining behavior. Simply, we act on the basis of how things seem to us. If the behavior of someone is to be understood, then, one of the first areas of attention is how things seem to him. Again, this seems so simple that it can be grossly misleading. What determines how things seem to us? The investigations into perception at the Hanover Eye Institute, conducted originally under the direction of Adelbert Ames and continued later by Hadley Cantril at Princeton, as well as recent studies of cognition under the direction of Jerome Bruner at Harvard reveal that the language we use greatly affects (if it does not completely determine) what we see and how we see it. On the basis of investigations conducted so far, the statement "Nothing is anything until you call it something and then it 'is' whatever you call it," could be well defended. Conversely, it is most difficult, if not impossible, to see "something" for which we do not have a name. Try to make a short list of "things" (items, relationships, processes) for which we have no names in English. You may find it impossible to do so.

What does psycholinguistics seem to be good for? To date it has served to unify diverse approaches to the study of human beings and what they do. Some feel that the interdisciplinary tenor of psycholinguistics is not unifying but disruptive, be-

THE LINGUISTIC ENTERPRISE–

	DIALECT STUDY	GRAMMAR	DESCRIPTIVE LINGUISTICS	LANGUAGE HISTORY
1900				
1910				George Krapp
1920				Otto Jespersen
1930		Henry Sweet H. Poutsma	Edward Sapir	Henry Wyld
1940	H. L. Mencken	George Curme Otto Jespersen Charles C. Fries	Leonard Bloomfield Kenneth Pike	Leonard Bloomfield
1950	Hans Kurath	Zellig Harris	Martin Joos Bernard Bloch George Trager Edgar Sturtevant George Trager & Henry Lee Smith Jr.	Albert Marckwardt
1960	G. Brooks Raven McDavid	George Trager & Henry Lee Smith Jr. Harold Whitehall Paul Roberts Noam Chomsky W. Nelson Francis Archibald A. Hill James Sledd Eugene A. Nida Robert B. Lees	Zellig Harris Henry A. Gleason Roman Jakobson Morris Halle Charles Hockett	Samuel Moore Albert Baugh John Firth Henry Hoenigswald
	Angus Macintosh Harold Orton	Emmon W. Bach J. Katz & Paul Postal Norman Stageberg	Andre Martinet	Winfred Lehmann Thomas Pyles

ITS MAJOR FIGURES

USAGE	LEXICOGRAPHY	SEMANTICS	PSYCHOLINGUISTICS
		Charles Peirce	
		Michel Breal Bertrand Russell	
		V. Welby Ludwig Wittgenstein	
H. W. Fowler Sterling Leonard	William Craigie	C. K. Ogden I. A. Richards Alfred N. Whitehead	Edward Sapir Jean Piaget H. Head
Herbert Horwill Arthur Kennedy Albert Marckwardt & Fred Walcott Charles C. Fries	William Neilson Allen W. Read Mitford Mathews C. Barnhart Harold Wentworth	Alfred Korzybski Rudolph Carnap A. J. Ayer Stuart Chase Hugh Walpole	L. S. Vygotsky
Robert Pooley Ernest Gowers		S. I. Hayakawa Irving Lee Charles Morris Wendell Johnson Susanne Langer Anatol Rapaport	Benjamin Lee Whorf Ernst Cassirer O. Hobart Mowrer George Miller
Bergen Evans & Cornelia Evans Robert Hall Jr.		Dorothy Lee S. Ullmann Benjamin Lee Whorf	L. A. Jeffress Charles Osgood Thomas Sebeok Eric Lennenberg J. M. Roberts Harry Hoijer Bronislaw Malinowski B. F. Skinner Roger Brown Joseph Church
Margaret Bryant	Philip Gove James Sledd		Sol Saporta John R. Carroll Edward Hall

cause it crosses clear disciplinary boundaries. You may note that there is a semantic or metalinguistic problem here.

The implications for education of such fields as metalinguistics and psycholinguistics are suggested by the approach taken in language training at the School of Language and Linguistics of the Foreign Service Institute. As the Institute catalogue puts it:

> Language is not considered as a mechanical tool but as a vital mode of communication with a people. Since language is an integral part of culture, the Institute's objective is to stress the language-and-culture unity and to develop insights on the part of the officer into the ways in which a foreign people thinks, feels, believes, and behaves —as well as talks and writes.

If language study were approached in this way in our schools generally, we might be able to achieve "cultural understanding" much more quickly than we now seem able to do. Moreover, one cannot help but wonder how differently problems in international relations, especially in Asia and Africa, might be handled if our political leaders understood some of the basic metalinguistic and psycholinguistic assumptions.

Psycholinguistics, at least in the forms it has taken in studies such as those done at Harvard's Center for Cognitive Studies, has already added several metaphors to the universe of discourse about education. Largely as a result of Jerome Bruner's writing, *A Study of Thinking* and *The Process of Education,* the use of such words as *structure, discovery, inductive,* and *intuition* are common in discussions of what and how to teach in the schools. To date, the seminal metaphor seems to be *structure*—referring to the "nature of the subject." Perhaps this is partly the product of the tendency to look mostly at "subjects," such as mathematics, that are closed systems. The next step in psycholinguistics may be to generate still another set of metaphors, enabling us to talk a bit more incisively about the psychology of the learner and his language, which, after all, determines for each individual learner what kind of "structure" a subject "has."

SELECTED BIBLIOGRAPHY

Beck, William S., *Modern Science and the Nature of Life.* New York: Harcourt, Brace and World, 1957.

Bloomfield, Leonard, *Language.* New York: Holt, Rinehart and Winston, Inc., 1965.

———, "Linguistics and Reading," *The Elementary Review,* XIX, April 1942.

Bridgman, P. W., *The Way Things Are.* Cambridge: Harvard University Press, 1959.

Bruner, Jerome, "Growth of Mind," *American Psychologist,* XX, December 1965.

Carlsen, G. Robert, "How Do We Teach?", *English Journal,* 1965.

Conant, James, *Modern Science and Modern Man.* New York: Columbia University Press, 1953.

Dewey, John, *How We Think.* New York: D. C. Heath and Co., 1933.

———, *Experience and Education,* the Kappa Delta Pi Lectures, 1938.

Dykema, Carl, "Historical Development of the Concept of Grammatical Properties," in *Readings in Applied English Linguistics* (edited by Harold Allen). New York: Appleton-Century-Crofts, 1958.

Encyclopedia of Educational Research (1950 edition). New York: The Macmillan Company.

Fries, Charles Carpenter, *American English Grammar.* New York: Appleton-Century-Crofts, 1940.

———, *Linguistics and Reading*. New York: Holt, Rinehart and Winston, Inc., 1962.

FROMM, ERICH, *May Man Prevail?*. New York: Doubleday and Co., 1961.

GARDNER, JOHN W., "Self-Renewal: The Individual and the Innovative Society," *Harper's*, 1964.

GLEASON, H. A., *Linguistics and English Grammar*. New York: Holt, Rinehart and Winston, Inc., 1965.

GRENE, MARJORIE, "Portmann's Thought," *Commentary*, November 1965.

HAYAKAWA, S. I., "Semantics, Law, and Priestly-Minded Men," *ETC.*, XIX, October 1962.

———, "Linguistic Science and the Teaching of Composition," *ETC.*, VII, Winter 1950.

JESPERSEN, OTTO, *Mankind, Nation and Individual*, First Midland Book Edition, 1964, by arrangement with George Allen and Unwin, Ltd., London.

JOHNSON, WENDELL, *People in Quandaries*. New York: Harper, 1946.

LAIRD, CHARLTON, *The Miracle of Language*. A Premier book, 1957.

LANGER, SUSANNE, *Philosophy in a New Key*. Cambridge: Harvard University Press, 1942.

LEES, ROBERT, "The Promise of Transformational Grammar," *English Journal*, May 1963.

LEFEVRE, CARL, *Linguistics and the Teaching of Reading*. New York: McGraw-Hill, 1964.

LEONARD, STERLING A., *Current English Usage*. Inland Press, 1932.

MALMSTROM, JEAN (with Annabel Ashley), *Dialects, U.S.A.*, NCTE, 1963.

MARCKWARDT, ALBERT, "Linguistics Issue: An Introduction," *College English*, January 1965.

MAUGHAM, W. SOMERSET, *The Summing Up*. New York: Doubleday & Co., 1938.

MINTEER, CATHERINE, *Words and What They Do to You*. New York: Row, Peterson, 1953.

MENNINGER, KARL (with Martin Mayman and Paul Pruysen), *The Vital Balance*. New York: The Viking Press, 1963.

NAGEL, ERNEST, "The Place of Science in a Liberal Education," *Daedalus*, 1959, Vol. 88, pp. 56–74.

OGDEN, C. K., and RICHARDS, I. A., *The Meaning of Meaning*. New York: Harcourt, Brace, 1923.

POOLEY, ROBERT, *Teaching English Usage*. New York: Appleton-Century-Crofts, 1946.

READ, ALLEN WALKER, "Linguists and the Sense of Mission," *ETC.*, Vol. XIX, October 1962.

RICHARDS, I. A., *Practical Criticism*. New York: Harcourt, Brace, 1929.

———, *Principles of Literary Criticism*. New York: Harcourt, Brace, 1925.

———, *Interpretation in Teaching*. New York: Harcourt, Brace, 1938.

ROBERTS, PAUL, "Linguistics and the Teaching of Composition," *English Journal*, May 1963.

RUSSELL, BERTRAND, *The Impact of Science on Society*. New York: Simon and Schuster, 1953.

SABOL, JAMES W., "An Experiment with Inductive Language Study" in *Patterns and Models for Teaching English* (edited by Michael Shugrue). NCTE, 1964.

SANDBURG, CARL, "Languages," from *Chicago Poems*. New York: Holt, Rinehart and Winston, Inc., 1916.

SAPIR, EDWARD, *Language: An Introduction to the Study of Speech*. New York: Harcourt, Brace, 1921.

———, "The Concept of Phonetic Law as Tested in Primitive Languages by Leonard Bloomfield," in *The Selected Writings of Edward Sapir* (edited by David G. Mandelbaum). Regents of the University of California, 1949.

WHITEHEAD, ALFRED NORTH, *The Aims of Education*. New York: The Macmillan Company, 1959.

WHORF, BENJAMIN LEE, "A Linguistic Consideration of Thinking in Primitive Communities," in *Language, Thought and Reality* (edited by John Carroll). Cambridge: Massachusetts Institute of Technology Press, 1956.

THIS BOOK WAS SET IN

BASKERVILLE AND TIMES ROMAN TYPES BY

BROWN BROS.

IT WAS PRINTED BY

THE MURRAY PRINTING COMPANY

AND BOUND BY

H. WOLFF BOOK MFG. CO., INC.

TYPOGRAPHY AND DESIGN ARE BY

BARBARA D. LIMAN.